Where's My Umbrella?

A Crash Course in Crisis Management

Len Biegel

Brick Tower Press
New York

Brick Tower Press
1230 Park Avenue
New York, New York 10128

© Len Biegel 2014

Library of Congress Cataloging-in-Publication Data
        Len Biegel
Where's My Umbrella?: A Crash Course in Crisis Management

Includes index.
ISBN: 978-1-883283-90-2
1. Biegel, Len—
Business/Economics
Insurance/Risk Assessment
Nonfiction

First Edition, September 2014

The opinions expressed in this book are solely those of the author and do
not represent those of any other entities, unless quoted.

Contents

Acknowledgments   v
Notes, Personal and Otherwise   vii
Introduction   xi

Part I: Are We Ready?

1: Do We Have a Crisis or Don't We?   9
2: What We Know   15
3: The Wake-Up Calls—Lessons Learned, Lessons Ignored   23
4: Denial in the Land of Risk   63
5: It's About CEO Leadership and Communication   69
6: The Media—Big Pluses, Big Minuses   81

Part II: Closing the Readiness Gap

7: A Prescription for 100 Percent Protection and Readiness   91

Part III: The Tool Kit

8: Tools You Can Use: A Guide to Commonly Used Terms   103
9: A Standard Approach to Crisis Planning   107
10: The Insider's Secrets to Good Crisis Planning   113
11: Validating the Crisis and Continuity Plans to Keep Them Alive   121
12: Ideas Beyond the Norm, or, "Why Aren't We Doing That?"   137

Index   144

This book is dedicated to Roberta, with deepest love.
And to the memory of Uncle Sidney. This book would not have been possible without his influence.

Acknowledgements

Never Say Never, the forerunner of *Where's My Umbrella?*, was born of influences, resources, and endless support. The acknowledgments are worthy of repeating here.

I am indebted to countless people at Royal Caribbean Cruises Ltd., and wish to express special thanks to Richard Fain, chairman and CEO, who sets a high standard for what crisis preparedness and response should be, and to Adam Goldstein, president of Royal Caribbean International, who first suggested, "You know, this is a book you should write"; to Carlos Campbell, who first introduced me to the National Association of Corporate Directors and has continued to be a welcome constructive critic; to Peter Gleason, NACD's chief operating officer, for his insights; and to Suzanne Hopgood, co-author of NACD's *Board Leadership for the Company in Crisis*, for her perspective and updates on how forward-thinking board members are addressing the crisis-preparedness issue.

Special thanks to my colleague Andy Gilman for his countless thoughtful comments and his insights into what Jim Burke was like as a student of media training; and to Aydin Caginalp, formerly of Alston & Bird LLP, who kindly offered to introduce me to John Colby, publisher of Brick Tower Press; and to John Colby, for his commitment and support.

And most of all, with love and appreciation to my sons—Adam, for his support, guidance and inspiration, which are matched only by his molecular-level attention to detail, and Jonathan, who shows a keen understanding of how business should serve its customers; and to my wife Roberta, who is able to see around corners, and inspires and supports with unconditional love.

Notes, Personal and Otherwise

In 1980, after several years in television (with CBS, Metromedia/Fox, and public broadcasting), followed by consulting for the Israel Broadcasting Authority, the Shah of Iran, and the North Atlantic Treaty Organization (NATO), I joined public relations firm Burson-Marsteller. The initial assignment was to create a media department for the Washington office that would help clients understand the often adversarial relationship between business and the media.

In the midst of this assignment, in 1982, Johnson & Johnson, the maker of the popular pain reliever Tylenol, received reports that several customers had died as the result of ingesting cyanide-laced Tylenol tablets.

As part of the small team assembled to help the client with the urgent and complex communications concerns, and having come from broadcasting, where we survived by understanding the public, I thought the answers were obvious: Be quick to respond, show you care about the public, do something about the problem, and explain it all through regular contact with the media. And with something this serious, put the CEO forth as the spokesperson. Well, that is exactly what Jim Burke, the chairman of J&J, did. In doing so, he proved that the public will understand and forgive an honest, caring CEO (whose company, by the way, was a victim of the crime, not the cause) who was bold enough to recall the entire retail supply of Tylenol and commit to the design of a tamper-proof pill and package. This swift, daring move worked. The brand eventually regained its market share, and the event marked the introduction of tamper-resistant packaging for almost all food and drug products.

Years later, clients still remark that the counsel given to Jim Burke was brilliant. No, I am quick to reply, it was our collective good sense, given an understanding of the public and the media. It highlights, most of all, what a leader can accomplish when he asks for advice, considers it, combines it with his best instincts, and moves quickly to protect his customers and products.

As with so many historic events—and this was without question a historic event—it takes time to realize its importance and to understand its long-term influence. As the dust began to settle—especially after it became clear that Tylenol in the tamper-proof bottles was regaining its place among consumers—questions began surfacing about what this all meant. As the months unfolded, several of us in the media end of the PR business began realizing that perhaps a company could prepare. Perhaps we could develop some criteria and rules for management and communication during a crisis.

The result: The management of the Tylenol tamperings of 1982 was a landmark for modern-day crisis management. It has become the textbook case for how to manage a crisis, and has spawned the modern-day profession of crisis management.

Well, stay tuned as we review the highs (and a few lows) of crisis communications and management over the past thirty-five years, and as we consider what the Tylenol moment of 1982, a succession of other, earlier business crises, and the milestones of 9/11 and other events mean for the CEO in today's vulnerable environment.

Much has happened on the political front over the past thirty years, with scandals, leadership ups and downs, and the like. And while it is tempting to comment on those important areas, that would require an entirely separate volume, so I let them pass—with three exceptions. I have chosen to comment on the leadership under the incredible stress of 9/11— that is, the leadership of former New York City Mayor Rudy Giuliani on 9/11; and NYC Mayor Michael Bloomberg and New Jersey Governor Chris Christis during Hurricane Sandy.

Crisis preparedness is not simply about guarding the front door, building a war room, creating a business continuity plan, or conducting a fire drill. It's about all of it and more!

If timing is everything—or nearly everything—we likely are entering a new and potentially constructive era for the modern corporation. This new era, the Era of Accountability, is marked by a number of trends that remind the corporations that they are accountable to their owners, the shareholders—whether these shareholders are the moms and pops hoping to increase their assets or the giant investment funds trusted by their shareholders to protect and grow their assets. These assets, whether one share or a million, are entrusted to boards of directors. The best board members are objective, smart, and experienced, and understand their fiduciary responsibilities to protect and grow the assets. The corporate scandals of the 1990s, highlighted by Tyco International, Enron, and MCI, will have a lasting effect if they spur scrutiny by the stock exchanges, government, and the shareholders in order to assure the most responsible board members.

An important new ingredient is growing on the governance to-do lists of many boards—and that is the protection of corporate reputation and assets through effective crisis prevention and readiness. If that trend continues, we are headed for the Never Say Never method of crisis management.

This shift toward accountability will not happen overnight. We have, in Part II, laid bare for the first time the steps needed to move from the gridlock in too many companies to Never Say Never readiness.

Introduction

Welcome to *Where's My Umbrella?*

Since the publication of *Never Say Never*, much has changed; and much has stayed the same. We have seen more cataclysmic weather-related events that, though not preventable, taught us the value of preparation. And we have witnessed more startling human events, such as the financial crisis, which could have been prevented had more attention been paid to early warnings. Cyber security now has risen to the top of the concerns, as hackers and phishers threaten our global information highway.

Where's My Umbrella? incorporates the best of *Never Say Never* while taking a fresh look at recent events, such as Hurricane Sandy and the financial crisis.

Never Say Never has been prelude to the events since publication five years ago. If only a crystal ball existed that could have predicted the superlatives that accompanied recent crises—the biggest Ponzi scheme; the biggest global financial crisis; the biggest oil spill; Hurricane Sandy, the biggest storm to hit the northeastern United States; Japan's catastrophic earthquake and nuclear problems; and the never-ending war on terror.

Despite tough challenges and tragic loss of life and property, the most resilient businesses, governments and communities pick up and renew, some sooner, some later.

As *Where's My Umbrella?* took shape, I reflected on the word "umbrella" and what it means for any business that may face multiple crises. It is a symbol of *protection* for a business and its reputation. And the umbrella brings together what for many companies are a number of efforts that should be *united* under one umbrella.

Despite the elimination of Osama bin Laden, the battle against terrorism continues, as we face an often-elusive enemy and search for new ways to communicate. Perhaps the most striking is the public campaign, "If you see something, say something."

In sharp contrast, the recent financial crisis has a well-defined set of adversaries, and yet change has been inexorably slow. Five-plus years after the financial crisis began, the accusations and blame still swarm across conference tables, reports, and some well-documented books; and some progress notwithstanding, the final government regulations and needed staffing are only beginning to take shape.

As crises ebb and flow, news media have become more mobile and more instant. Cell phones, smartphones and iPads deliver the news through Google alerts, emergency text messages, tweets, and apps a click away from the full paper or TV source.

With the increase in the number of ways we can receive news, the overall consumption or attention to news has increased. According to the Pew Research Center's September 2010 report, roughly a third of the public say they went online for news yesterday—on par with radio, and slightly higher than daily newspapers. And when cell phones, e-mail, social networks, and podcasts are added, 44 percent of Americans say they received news through one or more Internet or mobile digital sources yesterday. What is interesting, according to the Pew research, is that ". . . instead of replacing traditional news platforms, Americans are increasingly integrating new technologies into their news consumption habits."

More than a third of Americans say they received news from both digital and traditional sources yesterday, just shy of the number who relied solely on individual sources. For many of us, the new technologies provide choices that we turn to as supplements or replacements for traditional sources.

In some ways, the traditional sources, such as local TV news, are their own worst enemy. Simple example: If the 10 P.M. TV promotional headlines come on with "Forecast of heavy changes in the weather coming. Details at 11," I don't wait till 11. I turn to Yahoo Weather on the computer and get the story in seconds—and then turn off the TV and go to bed. The eleven o'clock news lost a viewer.

The traditional news media have been challenged as never before, as newspaper readership and TV news fight for readers and viewers. In the wake of all this, some newspapers have gone out of business or downsized. Most print media websites are constantly updated. One almost cannot distinguish between a TV newsroom and the local paper.

Those media that will survive understand innovation. The *New York Times* appears to be leading in innovation, as its website brings both print and video to the public in a totally user-friendly format.

While millions continue to rely on the traditional news media, especially in a crisis, each new advance in the digital world erodes or challenges that leadership. The ease of transmitting photos and short videos from our mobile cameras has created the citizen journalist who becomes the news source for the traditional media. And Twitter has gone beyond the original joke of "Who cares what you had for breakfast?" to become a growing source for news—whether the reporting of a crisis before the traditional media are aware of it, or the amplification of news as tweets re-tweet and recommend that, "Hey, you ought to check this out."

As the world is a-twitter with tweets, content still is king. Without content, the short bursts of news are nothing.

At the end of the day, the news media that will survive are the media that figure out how to make money in the digital space, are credible, and are sensitive to the time the public can devote to reading, listening, and viewing.

More than thirty years ago, the management of the Tylenol tampering crisis was held out as the icon for crisis response—fast, substantive reaction, and a caring company chairman as chief decider and spokesperson. Though the company faces other challenges today and the digital world has changed the way news travels, the Tylenol case still resounds with the "do the right thing" advice: Take responsible actions and take them quickly, and prepare and send out the best spokesperson you possibly can identify. He or she may not make as many TV appearances today, but his or her voice can and will be heard on tweets and YouTube and all the media online, up to the second.

Will the lessons of the recent past provide an impetus for prevention?

The Madoff meltdown could have been prevented if the Securities and Exchange Commission had heeded the warnings. The British Petroleum (BP) oil spill could have been prevented if BP and its contractors had listened to the safety warnings. The global financial crisis could have been prevented if all of the government regulators had been awake. And the capsizing of the *Costa Concordia* cruise ship did not need to happen.

Some Notes On Trends

I am often asked to predict the next big crisis. Most of us know that is impossible. But it is reasonably safe to identify some trends:

• The buck stops in the board room. Accountability is rising, as board members at publicly traded corporations are being encouraged to question their companies' readiness.

• Resiliency. The companies that will survive and thrive—large or small—are the ones that minimize bureaucracy and complacency, learn from experience, and react to change quickly.

• Planning for the worst. The best crisis plan is one that is easily accessible and brief—on a card in your wallet or an app on your smartphone or iPad . . . or both. The hundred-page crisis plan in a binder remains an important document as a policy guide and text for new members of a crisis team.

• The best crisis is the one that never happens. Crisis prevention has great value. The companies or institutions that are committed to simulations and planning will reap the added benefits of finding ways to prevent or diminish the possibility of a crisis.

• Attention-getters. The events of 9/11, the BP oil spill, the Murdoch and Madoff scandals, Hurricane Katrina, Hurricane Sandy, and the Japanese earthquake, tsunami and nuclear meltdown have further defined and refined the crisis management craft. Early warnings, crisis planning, and risk communications are gaining attention.

• CSR is on the rise. Corporate Social Responsibility challenges are rising around the globe, stimulated in large part by cheap labor in factories and farms where big-name products—from iPads to chocolate—are made. From China to the Ivory Coast, the conditions present an increasing challenge to "do the right and humane thing."

• Media. Today, crises can be illuminated with 140 characters via Twitter, triggering rapid, viral spread. Social media and iPads, Droids, and other mobile devices proliferate. This is making it easier for the average person to consume news and be a citizen journalist. Interestingly, the ability to consume news on the go is not diminishing the consumption of news on the traditional (or "legacy") media. The public is now consuming more and more news. The most resilient of the traditional media, such the *New York Times*, are in the forefront of the reinvention of the media.

- Dialogues increase. Current worst-case fears—including terrorism, data breaches, and riots and demonstrations—have raised concerns throughout the world. Organizations are concerned about trading best practices to prevent or cope with these events. One new organization has arisen to help: the Global Risk Network.

Imagine, if you will, that you are awakened from a deep sleep at 2 A.M. on Saturday. An automated emergency call system the company has recently subscribed to delivers the following message:

"This is the Action Plus Network with an urgent message. If this is Joe Doe, please enter your password, followed by the pound sign."

You follow instructions and hear the following:

"This is the Action Plus Network Emergency Line for Five-Star Uniform Company. This call is to notify you that there is an emergency situation requiring your immediate presence at the Corporate Situation Room. If you are receiving this message and will be proceeding to the Situation Room, please press star, then hang up. If you need further assistance, please press nine."

You dress quickly and head for the office, which is about twenty minutes away. As you are driving, you switch on the radio and hear the news that explosions have hit several international businesses. As many as two hundred textile workers have been killed in a massive fire in Bangladesh.

You are the CEO of Five-Star Uniform Corporation, the largest maker of uniforms for the United States military. The company has been the subject of mounting criticism over its outsourcing of garment assembly to China and Bangladesh. Despite a "Made in America" pledge required by the Department of Defense, the company has persisted in the outsourcing, and has received major press criticism.

This is just the beginning of a crisis you thought you were prepared to face. But are you prepared?

As the 9/11 Commission concluded, "We must begin to imagine future disasters, perhaps multiple catastrophes, for they, too, may well occur." The most important failure, the report concluded, was one of imagination.

Since 9/11, countless government agencies and trade associations have created well-intentioned "do this, do that" guides. But the sheer volume is daunting, if not confusing. Add to that the years of accumulated advice from those in the trenches of management—especially Jack Welch and Andy Grove—some of whose advice is included in this book.

What needs sorting out is what's out there and what is most useful for you and your company. This all assumes you want to improve your crisis readiness. And then there's the group of companies that do little or nothing and intend to coast along. Well, that's where we get into the tough part: how to instill a crisis-readiness culture everywhere it belongs—and it does belong everywhere. It's not going to happen because more to-do lists pop up. It will happen because there are pressures, accountability, and incentives—and we address that in this book as well.

The central themes of the book include the following:

• The shocking events of 9/11 and hurricanes Katrina and Sandy showed, above all, the value of planning for crisis response and business continuity. And, from a CEO point of view, the urgent need to take charge of the process.

• Are we as prepared as we should be? Not by a long shot! We're getting better. Will it take more wake-up calls? Or will it take commitment? It's up to you.

• The executive traits required in a crisis are the same as the best traits required during non-crisis periods. The difference is that, in a crisis, you are working at warp speed and under enormous pressure.

• Preparedness is a far better business choice than denial—and the second half of the book will detail the steps any company can and should take to be prepared.

• The best crisis is the one that never happens. While natural disasters will continue to challenge us and even increase, the human side of the crisis equation presents an opportunity to find ways to spot early warnings and avoid crises.

Who is this book for?

This book is for every CEO, every board member, and every senior executive concerned about corporate reputation, in companies of all sizes—from the Fortune 500s to the small- and medium-size companies—that do business with and are part of the private-sector supply chain that controls 85 percent of America's resources.

One may wonder why this book is aimed toward such a broad cross section of American business. The answer is simple. We are all in the same boat, sharing a common set of threats and concerns in today's world. While every company has specific concerns, we have reached the point where we all have more in common than not—and that is what this book is based on.

There is a great deal of specific activity under way across industries—from banking to chemicals—working to help protect their physical assets. What this book is about is how to protect the other asset—reputation, and how, in a worst-case situation, operations and market share must be protected with business continuity plans. Lose or weaken your reputation, and the consequences are as deep as and often deeper than any other loss. At the end of the day, it is about senior executive responsibility and accountability.

Part I

Are We Ready?

1: Do We Have a Crisis or Don't We?

When written in Chinese, the word crisis *is composed of two characters. One represents danger, the other opportunity.*

—John Fitzgerald Kennedy

Hold on! Do you even have a crisis? Not every event is a crisis. Regardless of the company, industry, location or size, every crisis, emergency, and issue share common features. Let's get some definitions straight:

Crisis: A major event, generally characterized by one or more of the following:

- Possible or actual harm to individuals or property, including computer networks
- Imminent threat to "business as usual"
- Imminent threat to company or brand reputation
- National or international media attention—either immediate or potential

Emergency: A situation that is localized and controllable, such as a fire or injury. It generally is characterized by one or more of the following:

- Local media attention
- No substantial or uncontrollable threat to individuals or property
- Little or no disruption to operations
- No threat or indication of problems beyond the specific location

Issue: A controversy, generally characterized by:

- Warnings through any number of sources—e.g., activist groups, legal claims, government investigations, research announcements, etc.
- Sufficient time to develop strategies and steps which may solve the problem before it escalates to a crisis
- No immediate harm or disruption to business

An issue is not a crisis.

Reactions to Crises

At the first signs of a crisis, reactions may be:

Denial—"This can't be happening."

Complacency—"If I ignore it, it may go away."

Blame—"Who would dare do this?"

All of the above are perilous and the wrong approach to take, though many companies do just that. The reality is that, as the old saying goes, "Where there's smoke, there's fire." The sooner the fact-finding begins, the sooner the strategies for some solutions can take shape. This requires a mindset that is willing to admit that something is wrong and that it is the company's responsibility to take charge—after all, if you don't, someone else will. And you will not like the results.

Successful crisis response requires:

• A plan

• Training and simulations

• Decisive leadership, combining rapid, thoughtful strategies and calm, well-tuned reactions—to get the facts, make decisions and act on them, and communicate to everyone concerned. But this takes some work.

While each event or crisis is different, or at least has different nuances and twists or turns, an effective crisis plan provides the framework for tackling any situation.

Soon after the Department of Homeland Security was formed, we began hearing a new phrase, "all hazards"—an important phrase to remind us that, though terrorism is the new big worry, we cannot and should not forget all the other hazards.

We live in a more complex world, which by definition carries more risks of possible disasters—from terrorism to widespread disease to natural disasters and hate crimes.

Are there telltale signs that a crisis is coming?

The answer is yes/maybe. Most crises take you by surprise. Others just might be on the horizon and can be spotted. It is worth considering some of the signs:

• Is there a nagging issue that simply will not go away?

• Are there mounting complaints and agitation on customer or activist blogs?

• Has an investigative reporter called, alleging some irregularities?

• Is there a competitor in the midst of a crisis?

• Are employee suggestions being ignored?

• Have budget concerns led to technical or procedural shortcuts?

An important note about terrorism

According to Rudy Giuliani, "Part of the damage the terrorists hope to inflict is the emotional reaction in the wake of the destruction. The reason it's called 'terrorism' is that they want fear and its debilitating effects to linger long after the smoke has cleared. By preparing citizens for the possibility of a terrorist attack," Giuliani adds, "leaders can help minimize the emotional response in the wake of the destruction." (Rudolph W. Giuliani, "Lessons of London: What's Next in War of Terror?" *USA Today*, July 11, 2005)

In 2005 the Homeland Security Council, a federal advisory body to the Department of Homeland Security, listed fifteen nightmares. Take a look at the following scenarios:

Nuclear Detonation: Nuclear device. Terrorists drive a van with a ten-kiloton nuclear device into the central business district of a major city and set it off.

Biological Attack: Aerosolized anthrax terrorists spray aerosolized anthrax from a van in three cities initially, followed by two more cities shortly afterward.

Biological Disease Outbreak: Flu pandemic—an influenza pandemic begins in south China and spreads within months to four major cities in the United States.

Biological Attack: Pneumonic plague terrorists release pneumonic plague into an airport bathroom, a sports arena, and a train station in a major city, and it spreads rapidly.

Chemical Attack: Blister agent terrorists in a small aircraft spray a chemical blister agent over a packed college football stadium.

Chemical Attack: Toxic industrial chemicals terrorists attack oil refineries with grenades and bombs; exploding cargo containers ignite ships, including one carrying toxic chemicals.

Chemical Attack: Nerve agent terrorists release sarin gas into the ventilation systems of three large office buildings in New York City.

Chemical Attack: Chlorine tank explosion terrorists infiltrate an industrial storage facility and blow up a storage tank of chlorine, releasing a large quantity of the gas.

Natural Disaster: Major earthquake—a 7.2-magnitude earthquake occurs on a fault line through a major city, affecting six counties with a total population of 10 million.

Natural Disaster: Major hurricane—a Category 5 hurricane with sustained winds of 160 miles per hour and storm surges of twenty feet hits a major metropolitan area.

Radiological Attack: "Dirty bombs" terrorists set off bombs with radioactive cesium 137 in three nearby moderate to large cities, contaminating thirty-six blocks in each.

Explosives Attack: Improvised bombs terrorists use handmade bombs, a large car or truck bomb, and suicide belts to attack a sports stadium and an emergency room.

Biological Attack: Food contamination terrorists use liquid anthrax to contaminate batches of ground beef and orange juice that are distributed to different parts of the country.

Biological Attack: Foot-and-mouth disease terrorists infect farm animals at several locations with foot-and-mouth disease, which spreads as the affected animals are transported.

Cyber Attack: Over a period of several weeks, terrorists conduct cyber attacks on several parts of the nation's financial infrastructure.

(Homeland Security Council,
reported in the *New York Times*, March 16, 2005)

This interesting and frightening list could expand, but it does illustrate the range of cataclysmic events we could face. In fact, hurricanes Katrina and Sandy were predicted rather accurately. If this list does not wake us to at least thinking about disaster and the consequences for business, what else will?

Are we prepared to face all these disasters? No. Would we collectively rise to the occasion? Yes, Americans are resilient and have a collective sense of responsibility in a disaster. We collect money; we donate food and clothing; companies send goods and services; fire departments, rescue squads, and hospitals all help each other. While there is ample evidence that more companies and organizations, and local, state, and federal agencies are better prepared since 9/11, we never can prepare for everything. But can we do a better job? Yes.

We can do a better job by:

• Closing the readiness gap, bringing the unprepared into the realm of the prepared.

• Creating a professional association concerned with setting standards, conducting training, and sharing best practices in crisis preparedness.

• Holding CEOs and others accountable for preparedness.

More on this in *Part II: Closing the Readiness Gap.*

2: What We Know

In the post-9/11, post-Katrina/Sandy world, we are faced with new regulatory threats, greater uncertainty, more complex risks, globalization, and the 24/7 news cycle.

Crisis management as we know it today emerged after the Tylenol tamperings of the mid-1980s. While there are no "official" standards yet for effective crisis management, generally accepted standards have evolved over several years as a direct result of the public handling of the Tylenol case. Faced with sustained, unprecedented media coverage of this crime against an American icon, public affairs professionals began reflecting almost immediately on what this all meant: Could companies prepare for a crisis? Could they all do as well as Johnson & Johnson CEO Jim Burke did in handling a crisis? Could a crisis in fact be prevented?

Since the Tylenol event, U.S. and global businesses have faced a host of crises of all dimensions. Some have been managed successfully—with success directly linked to the survival of corporate and brand reputation and/or market share. Others have failed spectacularly, with some of the worst involving the departure of the CEO. In a few remarkable cases, we have actually seen the demise or severe restructuring of entire companies, such as Enron, Union Carbide, A.H. Robins, and Tyco International, to name a few.

How well prepared are we? Or are we not?

The global preparedness picture remains grim. A Penn Schoen Berland survey of large and small businesses across the globe conducted in June 2011 showed that 54 percent have a plan and 46 percent do not have a plan. Of those with plans, 47 percent see gaps in their plans. A 2011 survey of U.S. and Canadian businesses conducted by FleishmanHillard showed that, of those companies with plans, only 29 percent update it once a year.

Who is prepared? The bigger the company, the better the readiness picture. Ninety-seven percent of the Fortune 200 companies have an emergency response plan that has been updated since the 9/11 terrorist attacks. Nearly 90 percent of the companies test their emergency plans each year, and 40 percent test their plans at least twice each year. Three of the best-prepared companies are Walmart, Tiffany & Company, and Royal Caribbean Cruises LTD.

The area most improved since 9/11 is technology. While not perfect, it is far better than before. The financial industry has made heavy investments in avoiding redundancy and protective measures to keep our banks and stock exchanges running in the event of an attack. This is encouraging in light of the essential role technology plays in our economy, and as an antidote to the oft-mentioned motives of the terrorist who sees our economy as a prime target. On other levels, such as physical security and access to buildings and plants, there is a checkerboard of systems, from some highly secure buildings in New York City, to the virtual fortress surrounding Washington's House and Senate offices, to virtually nothing in office buildings in some cities.

Succession planning presents another big void. If the CEO suddenly cannot function, for reasons of health or other absence, someone needs to take over immediately. According to a survey by Korn/Ferry International, more than 60 percent of companies worldwide do not have a capable CEO-in-waiting. ("Most Major Corporations Unprepared for Potential Succession Needs, According to Global Survey Of Recruiters," press release, Korn/Ferry International, May 3, 2005)

Globalization has created vast new markets, and outsourcing key functions such as call centers and data processing has become the norm. But challenges abound that, if left unchecked, could open the door to crises.

Consider, for example, that only half the offshore organizations use passwords for entry to data systems they are managing. (In contrast, 78 percent of U.S. organizations have strict password rules.) And 50 percent admit that more than half their users are not in compliance with their information security policies.

The result: Extortion, fraud and intellectual property theft have risen to the top of the list of concerns.

And finally—we are not alone. Until 9/11, American companies had not experienced an act of terror on U.S. soil. Nations around the world have become increasingly concerned since 9/11. England has had its share of terror scares and attacks, but no other nation has been struck by more bombings and continued to function at top speed than Israel.

My family and I lived in Israel for six months several years ago. What was striking was the way security was and still is a part of life. Briefcases and purses were searched when entering a bank, a large shop, a movie theater, or a museum. Soldiers were everywhere, carrying submachine guns on the streets. Radios played in the buses, delivering the latest news for all. But life went on; security is a way of life.

Eyal Kaplan. general partner, Walden Israel Venture Capital, summed up crisis readiness among Israeli businesses: "[M]aybe military training makes us defiant. We have to prove to the world that they made a mistake when they didn't invest in Israel because of the terrorist situation. And every businessperson I know feels the same way. We are driven to show the world how good we are, especially during times of crises.

"Here, we are all in this together," he continued. "In Israel, we are a group-oriented culture. Always be a David in attitude, even though you may be a Goliath in assets."

Israel has been guarding the country's assets so long that its security is often looked at as a model. Danny Halpern, a financial consultant in Israel, put it this way: "If we have one guard in front of a mall that has been bombed, America will put up ten guards before the people are reassured. Here, I believe we invest more in the quality of our security people and less in the mechanics. In America, because of the huge numbers, the investment is in the mechanics—the system—and then they hire minimum-wage security staff. Here it's the opposite." (Dan Carrison, *Business Under Fire*, Amacom, 2004)

Amid the indicators of business preparedness, or lack of it, some rather odd polling numbers have appeared that show that the general public thinks the nation is better prepared for events such as a pandemic or another terrorist attack than it really is. In survey results released by Columbia University in February 2007, 46 percent of those surveyed said the nation has become better prepared in the last year. Dr. Irwin Redlener, director of the National Center for Disaster Preparedness at Columbia's Mailman School of Public Health, was stunned by the results. "There is no basis in reality for saying we're better off than we were a year ago, and nothing about our political, functional environment should give anybody any confidence that it's improved." (Richard Perez-Pena, "A Perception of Progress on Disaster Preparedness," *New York Times*, February 20, 2007)

How You Communicate is at the Core

The news media thrive on chaos. And news travels at the speed of light. Technology is changing the rules of journalism, enabling anyone to report news on the web or send reports, photos, and videos to traditional news outlets. This all doubtless will have some affect on journalism—though time will tell how and to what extent, as the public makes choices on how it perceives all this information.

When a crisis hits, stand up and be counted—in the first minutes if possible. If not, others will start speaking up and interpreting, speculating and guessing. And you may never catch up. Look, for example, at the stable of "experts" CNN and the other news outlets have on tap to comment in crises. They may be experienced people, but they generally have no knowledge at all about your crisis. They are simply speculators.

Open communication leads to trust, and trust is what you need in a crisis—from employees, customers, shareholders, and lawmakers. As Harold Burson, founder of Burson-Marsteller, puts it, "By taking the offensive and addressing the concerns, real and imagined, of key audiences, a company is more likely to be viewed as a responsible and responsive citizen rather than a recalcitrant or indifferent monolith." ("Crisis Management," undated white paper)

What You Need to Do

Crisis management professionals know that companies who do better in a crisis are those that:

• Stop looking for excuses and commit to planning.

Eric Holdeman, director of emergency management for Seattle's King County (an area prone to a significant earthquake threat), put it this way:

"There are four stages of denial. One is, it won't happen. Two is, if it does happen, it won't happen to me. Three: If it does happen, it won't be that bad. And four: If it happens to me and it's bad, there's nothing I can do to stop it anyway." (Amanda Ripley, "Why We Don't Prepare for Disaster," *Time*, August 20, 2006)

Jack and Suzy Welch offer some advice based on Jack's years of experience at General Electric:

"First, assume that the problem is worse than it appears. Skip the denial step, and get into the mindset that the problem will get bigger, messier, and more awful than you can possibly imagine.

"Second, assume there are no secrets in the world and that everyone will eventually find out everything.

"Third, assume you and your organization's handling of the crisis will be portrayed in the worst possible light. Define your own position early and often.

"Fourth, assume there will be changes in processes and people. Almost no crisis ends without blood on the floor.

"Fifth, assume your organization will survive, ultimately stronger for what happened." (Jack Welch and Suzy Welch, *Winning*, HarperCollins, 2005)

• Embrace an all-hazards approach to crisis planning. If the events of 9/11, the capsizing of the *Costa Concordia* cruise ship, or the floods of Hurricane Sandy taught us anything with regard to risk analysis, it is that the unthinkable can happen. Smart companies are eliminating the complex probability analyses and looking at all risks equally. They ask the same tough question of each risk: If this happened here, are we prepared?

• Understand that the war on terrorism is a long-term battle, and may directly or indirectly affect any company at any time. Frances Frago Townsend, former assistant to the President for Security and

Counterterrorism, put it this way: "When you talk about the threat, you have to talk about the enemy. The enemy is fractured, it is degraded, but it's not less lethal. I think it's important that people understand that. We worry about the aviation threat. When you look at things like the London plot—you know, it's funny, it's been termed the 'London plot,' but that's clearly a misnomer because, while the launching point for it was London, it was a plot directed at the United States, at killing U.S. citizens and causing U.S. economic damage and fracturing the relationship of a critical ally in Great Britain. So we know that if anyone needed proof of the continued threat, August [2006] should have been it." (David W. Silverberg, "Assessing the Threat," *HS Today*, January, 2007)

• Understand that effective crisis management requires leadership—and this includes your commitment to direct responsibility for both crisis readiness and response should a crisis occur. This means that readiness is not a sometime, expendable activity. In the most effective companies, it is a required responsibility. While many companies have effective crisis plans in place, there is also ample evidence to suggest that for many it remains a sometime activity, simulations and training are easily postponed, or the crisis preparation function is not coordinated at a senior level.

• Show they care about their employees, customers, shareholders and the public.

We know, for example, that following an explosion or a fire or natural disaster, employees and their families need to connect quickly to know they are safe. When faced with situations in which people lack control of the environment, such as a nuclear power plant exposure, we are able to call on the well-researched concepts of effective risk communication.

• Openly and quickly share the facts—good and bad—with their customers and the public.

• Accept blame when they are at fault.

• Continuously examine their vulnerabilities and find possible ways to prevent crises.

• Prepare and practice.

• Learn from mistakes—theirs and those of others.

But . . . to what degree are the CEO and other senior execs involved?

I was asked not long ago by the CEO of a Fortune 50 company to tell him what I thought he ought to do to assure that his company is crisis-ready.

The answer:

Assume personal responsibility for making sure that the company is crisis-ready.

Make certain that all plans are as short as possible. (In fact, the best plan should fit in your shirt pocket and on your smartphone or iPad.)

Make a commitment to practice, practice, practice, practice!

While some CEOs have assumed more direct responsibility for crisis preparedness and response, some companies or industries persist in sheltering the CEO from the realities of what could be massive threats to the organization. In the airline industry, for example, the tradition had generally called for the CEO to avoid any public appearances—especially before the media—when a crash occurred, until many hours had passed, and there was some evidence of the cause. This began to change in response to the events of 9/11. In another example, this involving a drug company, the rule at one time was to avoid letting the CEO know of any product-related deaths until a magic number of six or more had been reached.

Share price is always a big concern—even bigger when a crisis strikes. According to a report by the Corporate Executive Board, "The willingness of the financial community to punish missteps is attention-getting, but would not raise a serious alarm if the stock price damage were temporary." The study found that 41 percent of the companies that experienced a shock (i.e., a 30 percent decline) to their share price took a year to recover. But 32 percent never recovered. ("Refocusing Reputation Management," The Corporate Executive Board, 2004)

Reputation matters, especially in the eyes of Wall Street. A clear majority—88 percent—of analysts say reputation is important. It is scored even a shade higher in Europe, with 91 percent emphasizing the importance, and yet higher—94 percent— by analysts in Asia and the Pacific. (Hill & Knowlton Corporate Reputation Watch, May 31, 2006)

An ounce of prevention pays big dividends.

Prevention is possible if you have tight procedures and ethics standards, and review them regularly and enforce them. Training plays a big role in all of this—so that everyone, without exception, knows the rules of the road. Listen to employees for prevention ideas—in the old suggestion box or in its new electronic forms. Look at drills as a template for identifying areas that can be changed or improved, preventing a crisis.

The speed at which change can occur today, and the impact it can have, increases the need for crisis planning. "The speed and broader impact of change increases business risk and reduces viable reaction time. This makes preparing for change and crisis more critical than ever—especially since corporations are often judged more harshly for their responses to a crisis rather than the fact that they had a crisis in the first place." (Report of the NACD Blue Ribbon Commission on Risk Oversight, 2002, 2003, 2006)

Special interest and activist organizations know how to attract attention. Even the threat to harm a brand's market share through boycotts and other exploits will often call a company to action. While most boycotts have only succeeded in causing considerable angst for companies, there are a few that do stand out for having achieved their goals. For example, pressure on McDonald's by the National Heart Savers Association forced reduction in the use of fats in some of its fried foods, and led to changes in menu options. Animal activists nearly destroyed the fur coat industry through boycotts and public demonstrations. Ongoing opposition to bioengineered foods in Europe and the United States has limited the growth of this emerging technology. And, most recently, shareholder activists played a big role in the ouster of Bob Nardelli as CEO of The Home Depot.

The tweets and blogs are here, with enormous potential to help spot problems early on. Just think of the power of consumers or activists to create tweets and blogs telling of problems or perceived injustices and, in worst-case situations, to spread rumors and threats.

3: The Wake-Up Calls
—Lessons Learned, Lessons Ignored

Sept. 11 and Katrina brought calls to build impregnable walls against such tragedies ever occurring again. But despite the vows, both New Orleans and the nation's security apparatus remain dangerously leaky. "People call these crises 'wake-up calls,' " says Dr. Irwin Redlener, associate dean of Public Health at Columbia University and director of the National Center for Disaster Preparedness. "But they're more like snooze alarms. We get agitated for a while, and then we don't follow through."
("Why We Worry About The Things We Shouldn't," by Jeffrey Kluger, *Time*, December 4, 2006)

The crises described in the following pages are a cross section of high profile crises and a few lesser known ones. They each have been chosen to illustrate important lessons learned, but are not intended as an encyclopedia of crises.

The *Big* Wake-Up Calls: 9/11, Katrina, and Sandy

"Nothing surprises me after September 11, 2001. I think I took that word out of my vocabulary after that incident." —Rudy Giuliani

September 11, 2001, was one of those crystal-clear, sunny days, a seemingly perfect day on the East Coast. Washington, D.C., traffic was heavy that day; I arrived at the office a bit later then usual and was welcomed by about a half dozen staff members standing in front of the TV set in front of my desk. They were gazing in horror at the scene on CNN showing the World Trade Center with smoke pouring from one of the towers. Neither they nor CNN knew what really had happened. The phone rang a moment later, with a call from client American Airlines. "We don't know what's going on, but we're going to need help. Could you get staff to Dulles, JFK, and LAX to stand by in case they're needed?"

The wheels were set in motion immediately, and we worked through the next hours and days helping American Airlines with logistics and communications. There was no turning back. This was a moment that would change America.

"We are entering a period in which a small number of people, operating without overt state sponsorship but using the enormous power of modern computers, biogenetic pathogens, air transport, and even smaller nuclear weapons, will be able to exploit the tremendous vulnerabilities of modern societies." (Philip Bobbitt, "Get Ready for the Next Long War," *Time*, September 9, 2002)

On 9/11, lack of information about evacuation routes and procedures became a major hindrance to those who did try to escape. Though much had been done to assure safe building evacuations and fire safety in the wake of the Triangle Shirtwaist fire more than a century ago, it is shocking to realize that only 45 percent of 445 World Trade Center survivors had known the building had three stairwells. And only half knew the doors to the roof were locked.

The unprecedented events of 9/11, to a far greater degree than any disaster in U.S. history, provided another, showed that the unthinkable may occur. Katrina, by contrast, was predictable. It was only a matter of time until a Category 5 hurricane struck New Orleans and the Gulf region.

Then Hurricane Katrina, the nation's worst natural disaster, hit the Gulf region in 2005. It's been said that it was a miracle that so many companies have been able to function in the region. It's no miracle. Those that quickly resumed operations had plans.

While it is widely acknowledged that the federal government failed after Hurricane Katrina, many companies were able to activate their disaster plans and do a heroic job despite lack of electrical power and security. The biggest challenge, amid this backdrop of chaos, was how to help their employees put their lives back together. The plans that worked best—and these include those of The Home Depot, Walmart, BellSouth, Folgers, Oreck, and others—were detailed in every aspect. What made them work, too, is these companies' low tolerance for red tape, as well as can-do attitudes and strong support from their main offices.

A *Time* magazine poll one year later (August 20, 2006) found that only 16 percent of New Orleans' citizens said they were "very well prepared" for the next one. (Amanda Ripley, "Why We Don't Prepare for Disaster," *Time*, August 20, 2006)

One of the basic concerns in the wake of a hurricane is the massive structural damage to homes and businesses. While most states have strict building codes to protect against disasters, not all do. After Katrina, Louisiana looked at mandatory building codes, joining another hurricane-prone state, Florida. Florida's code, on the books since 2001, is generally believed to protect structures in winds as high as 120 mph. Mississippi, also hit by Katrina, still has no statewide code.

On the whole, big businesses fared better than the small ones, but few have come away without deep scars. Hotels, restaurants, and casinos, once the lifeblood of the city, have been slow to recover.

An inside look at FedEx's disaster preparedness system presents an interesting picture.

"Emergency central is a big, dimly lit room on the fourth floor of its new Global Operations Control in Memphis. John Dunavant is the GOC's chief; it's his job to make sure the hundreds of planes and thousands of trucks arrive when they're supposed to, and to have a sure-fire backup plan when they don't. A large screen at the front of the room shows the position, origin, and destination of every aircraft FedEx currently has in the sky. . . . [With] such events as an air-traffic-controller strike in France and blackout in Los Angeles . . . it's no wonder that FedEx gets so much practice in flexibility. What's more, FedEx conducts disaster drills several times a year—for everything from big earthquakes to bioterrorism to a monster typhoon hitting the company's hub in the Philippines. Eight disaster kits, each containing two tons of such supplies as fuel and communications gear, stand ready in Memphis in case a facility is in need of repair." (Ellen Florian Kratz, "For FedEx it Was Time to Deliver," *Fortune*, October 3, 2005)

The FedEx GOC became a major resource during Katrina—delivering ice, home generators, and water to Baton Rouge and Tallahassee, providing an enormous survival link for FedEx employees. And, like others, FedEx delivered countless shipments of emergency supplies for the Red Cross.

What did FedEx learn from all this?

As FedEx told CNN:

• Lesson No. 1: Arrange for temporary housing in advance for employees who might get displaced.

• Lesson No. 2: Don't count on cell phones. The local networks were down for days after the storm; the company is increasing the number of satellite phones it deploys. (CNN broadcast, October 2007)

One of the biggest lessons learned for all was that security is a big issue in a disaster like Katrina. In the desperate days following the storm, when the railroads, for example, placed portable generators at switching points, they were stolen within moments.

The much smaller Oreck, the maker of vacuum cleaners with a plant in the region, also had a plan and a strategy.

"If they were an Oreck employee before the hurricane, they still have a job," was the loud and clear declaration of Tom Oreck, the company's president and CEO. Against all odds, the company brought temporary housing, generators, food, water, and supplies to its employees in the region. By September 9, less than two weeks after the hurricane struck, the Gulfport plant, with five hundred employees, was up and running.

The secret? Oreck anticipated the worst and had plans in place. Before Katrina hit, the company had transferred its computer operations and call center to backup or continuity locations in Colorado. When the storm hit, it took two days to re-establish lost communications with employees.

Ingenuity played a role at Oreck and virtually every other company in the region. At Oreck, the fifteen-year-old son of the company's marketing vice president built a basic website allowing employees to post messages; and the company established a toll-free number employees could call for information and recorded messages from Tom Oreck.

In the hours and days that followed, everything from food and shelter to power was needed. Without power, the entire recovery effort was useless—and the Oreck team assigned to find generators found three in Miami, paying $250,000 for them.

Ironically, a year and half later, Oreck announced it would move the plant that survived so well to another part of the United States. "[Sixteen] months later, Oreck is throwing in the towel and moving its manufacturing to Tennessee. The company says it cannot get enough insurance to cover its Mississippi plant, and cannot hire enough skilled workers to replace those who never returned after the storm, mostly because they had nowhere to live.

" 'The decision to move this plant was a very difficult one, a very painful one,' said Oreck, the company president. But late last year 'we came to realize that conditions on the Gulf Coast had changed in ways that made doing business here very difficult.' " ("Oreck Comeback Effort Fails After Katrina," *Kansas City Star*, January 16, 2007)

The labor force in the New Orleans region is 30 percent smaller than it was prior to Katrina, according to a Brookings Institution study.

And finally—any discussion of Katrina would be incomplete without the mention of early warnings and bureaucracy, concerns prevalent throughout business. For more than ten years, it had been reported, scientists, media and Gulf area leaders had been warning that the day of the big and fatal hurricane was inevitable. Louisiana State University and University of New Orleans scientists had in fact created computer models showing that the impact of a hurricane had the real potential to overwhelm the levees. As the *New Orleans Time-Picayune* reported: "It's a matter of when, not if."

After:

While many of the old rules still apply, the events of 9/11 and Katrina continue to suggest additional urgent criteria:

Crisis management must be a full-time responsibility. Part-time, "when-I-get-to-it" assignments fall far short of the magnitude and urgency of the job.

The obvious is worth restating: As companies have faced crises over the years, those that have had solid, well-tested response and continuity plans fare better than those without plans.

Throw out the old notions of vulnerability assessment, which called for weighing the probability of each risk a company might face, and concentrating on planning for the most probable. If every risk is subjected to the tough questions ("Are we prepared?" and "Can we prevent this?"), then you can have a clear picture of your readiness. As former British Prime Minister Margaret Thatcher once offered: "The unexpected happens. You had better prepare for it."

Plan for business continuity as if your survival depended on it. Dozens of smart companies in the Gulf region were able to continue essential services through alternate locations and to resume operations as quickly as possible.

Regular crisis simulations are enormously helpful and are essential. The results are a disciplined crisis team and the almost certain result that each simulation will lead to an improved procedure or reveal a step which can prevent a real crisis.

But more is needed—and that is a commitment to drills for the crisis team, and evacuation drills for all employees.

When an alarm sounds, the reaction most people seem to have when faced with an emergency is disbelief: This cannot be happening. "Michael Lindell, a professor at the Hazard Reduction & Recovery Center at Texas A&M University, observed that most people go their entire lives without a disaster. 'So,' he says, 'the most reasonable reaction when something bad happens is to say, "This can't possibly be happening to me." ' He sees the same reaction when large numbers of people are faced with an evacuation. People caught up in disasters tend to fall into three categories. About 10 to 15 percent remain calm and act quickly and efficiently. Another 14 percent or less lose control—weeping, screaming, or otherwise hindering the evacuation. But the vast majority does very little initially. They are stunned and bewildered." (Amanda Ripley, "How to Get Out Alive," *Time*, May 2, 2005)

Generally accepted standards for crisis management are urgently needed. The thousands of post-9/11, well-meaning guides, and the recent push for adaptation of NFPA 1600 (see Chapter 7), are not enough. The time has come for a national crisis institute that will house the standards, provide certifications and training, and act as the clearinghouse for best practices in crisis management.

And finally, the time has come to hold CEOs accountable for their crisis planning.

Think of how to calm your employees. And leadership counts. On 9/11, the leader was New York's Mayor Rudy Giuliani—whose physical presence and calming, strong words through the days and weeks following 9/11 lifted the spirits of everyone. How? It was his combination of decisiveness, candor, and compassion.

When the planes hit the World Trade Center and the horror was seen instantly on TV, businesses across the United States, whether affected or not, needed to calm jittery staffs. As Paul Argenti of Dartmouth College's Tuck School of Business put it, "In periods of upheaval, workers want concrete evidence that top management views their distress as one of the company's key concerns. Written statements have their place, but oral statements and the sound of the empathic human voice communicates sincerity. And if the voice belongs to a company leader, the listener has reason to think that the full weight of the company stands behind whatever promises and assurances are being made. In the words of Rob Densen, Oppenheimer's director of corporate affairs and a survivor of the 1993 bombing of the World Trade Center, most people engulfed in a crisis 'want to be led' and accordingly need to trust that you are going to lead them." ("Crisis Communications: Lessons from 9/11," Paul Argenti, *Harvard Business Review*, December 1. 2002)

Entergy, the power company in the path of Katrina, offered a "baker's dozen" of lessons learned—and here I am going to break the rule of No More than Three Key Messages (discussed later in this book), because this is so important.

(1) In a crisis, speed is not everything. Speed is the only thing.

(2) Create detailed communications plans covering all kinds of crises—and drill them.

(3) Have a pre-determined, pre-equipped command center. And get your first troops there fast.

(4) Make your own organizational decisions on issues like evacuation.

(5) Don't wait for government to act—that may be too late.

(6) Enforce "one voice" communications.

(7) Assume all normal communications methods will collapse; have backups ready. Toll-free lines and key cell phones need out-of-region area codes.

(8) Have lines of authority and approval processes set beforehand. Understand that employees—not customers—are your most important audience.

(9) Anticipate significant emotional strain.

(10) Good response and good communications go hand in hand—if one fails, they both fail.

(11) Take calculated risks—especially in dealing with the media. Abandon your conservatism.

(12) Learn from your mistakes.

(13) And finally—remember that the more prepared a company is, the less dependent it will be on local government resources, which may be overwhelmed in a disaster.

Change continues. Just a few examples:

Security has been tightened at office buildings and other sites across the United States. In an uneven checkerboard of procedures, visitors in some locations are met with procedures that require escorts, while in other locations a signature in the lobby—with no further proof of appointment or ID—is all that is required. The increased demand for security "officers" and the cost of wages and training continues to be a challenge.

Mail is being scanned before delivery throughout some buildings, creating a boom for e-mail and a big question mark about the future of "snail mail." The post-9/11 anthrax scare coincided with a downward spiral for "snail mail" in favor of e-mail, instant messaging, and FedEx and UPS.

Insurance against terrorism may also be available.

The web is our instant news source, while the great divide between the informed and the uninformed public grows, as does cynicism towards mainstream news media.

On a different note, 9/11 created deeper feelings of patriotism.

The Blackout of 2003

Fifty million businesses lost power in the United States and Canada in the Blackout of 2003, crippling a huge area of the northeastern and central United States. In some areas power was lost for two days.

New York City Mayor Michael Bloomberg, vowing to avoid another blackout, created a plan for the city that was put to the test during the intense heat of 2006. A crucial part of the post-2003 strategy was the creation of a database of private and government backup generators already in place for a variety of safeguards. When the city's power grid was once again strained in 2006, the government and private entities were told to switch to their standby generators, thus temporarily relieving the Con Ed grid of the pressure.

In addition, the plan called for an ongoing inventory of supplies, so that there would be an orderly distribution should they be needed.

And finally, in a bow to low-tech communications, the neighborhood conservation plan deployed sound trucks and door-to-door visits to large buildings, urging conservation of power with a simple message: raise thermostats during the heat spell and help conserve power.

After:
There was no Blackout of 2006.

Hurricane Sandy, the Superstorm of 2012

The hurricane path was predicted for several days in late October 2012, and there is ample evidence that businesses, government, and people in their homes took every reasonable precaution. However, no amount of last-minute preparation could have prevented the massive flooding.

Hurricane Sandy wrought the worst destruction along the eastern United States, with the worst havoc on the shores of New Jersey, coastal New York City, and Connecticut. With millions throughout some of the nation's most densely populated areas without power, and countless homes, businesses, and hospitals flooded, the worst nightmare had arrived. New York Harbor, the historic lifeblood of the city, showed how it could become the enemy, as the waters rose through the streets and into the lobbies, basements, and shops, and down the steps into the subway and into the tunnels connecting Brooklyn and New Jersey with Manhattan.

Despite the massive challenges, a resilient community of New Yorkers, New Jerseyites, and Connecticut residents and businesses joined, with help from others around the country, to rescue thousands of stranded people and help to begin the recovery. The repair and recovery will go on for years. As New Jersey Governor Chris Christie said, many parts of the region will never be the same again.

Since the superstorm, discussions began to turn to the need to evaluate climate change and how to better prepare for the next "big one." There is a massive, complicated set of concerns, from how government will decide or not to encircle the region with sea walls or other means, and how businesses especially will update or create response plans, change infrastructure, and create and test business continuity plans.

Forces of nature cannot be stopped. The challenges are how well we prepare, react, and recover. The purpose of this section on the superstorm of 2012 is to look at how we did, and, based on these lessons learned, look at the future.

Realities

Hurricanes are not new to the New York metro region. Hurricane Carol in 1954 brought major flooding; Donna in 1969 brought eleven-foot waves; and there were Connie and Agnes and Gloria. And, in 1995, Felix. While severe, none were of the force of Sandy.

Despite debates and some naysaying, our climate is changing and there is a growing body of research and experience that concludes that we are facing more weather calamities. Though the debate over climate change continues in some quarters, one thing is certain: Sea levels are slowly rising; storm surges thus are more likely to produce flooding.

Federal Government Response

Local and state governments—let's call them first responders—performed remarkable rescue and emergency services. Whether rescue squads, fire departments, or police, they were out in force.

Then came FEMA. In 2005, the Federal Emergency Management Administration (FEMA) was widely criticized in the aftermath of Hurricane Katrina for slow response, lack of leadership, and a host of other issues. This time, a new FEMA was in the spotlight. After Katrina, legislation was passed requiring that the FEMA administrator have experience in emergency response. Craig Fugate, the current administrator, fills that bill and earned praise from the respective governors. Despite the praise, some residents were understandably quick to plead for more, faster help.

"What's going on," said Fugate, "is part of a priority system. Search-and-rescue operations take priority over providing assistance, and searches are still going on," Fugate told CNN two days after the storm. Assistance for survivors "is being made," he said, "but we haven't reached everybody. Until we do, we're not stopping."

The big difference? FEMA was ready, with supplies, staff, and transportation, to move into the area as soon as it had the official state requests for help. Irwin Redlener, director of Columbia University's National Center for Disaster Preparedness, said that Fugate ". . . has been able to attract staff back into the agency, and they have a very competent midlevel management layer to help organize efforts. They're still probably underfunded, but their staffing is much, much better."

Included in FEMA's reorganization is a public statement that FEMA is not the superhero capable of doing everything. Under a concept it calls "Whole Community," FEMA emphasizes an ongoing approach that the most effective response to disasters is FEMA working with all levels of the community, including individuals.

Communications

"Many people measured their overall health and well-being not just by how they were doing physically, but by a new standard: the percent of battery life left on their smartphone or tablet. Walking around the affected areas, you would ask people how they were doing and almost immediately people would say, "I'm doing all right, but I've only got 12 percent battery left on my phone."

With no power to charge phones and cell towers knocked out in most places, mobile phone connections were irregular for days. Text messaging fared better when you had battery power, and tweets became a widely used information source. Twitter became the "pop-up town square." You could get short bursts of news about what a mayor said in a press conference, what the power companies were predicting for restoration of power, where to find an alternate voting location, and what the next day's weather might bring. You could get news of colleagues, friends, and relatives, and business pushed out information to customers—where ATMs were working, where food markets were open.

But if you were told to work from home—as many were told in the first few days after the storm—it often was impossible without power.

People Helped People; Businesses Helped Businesses

The worst brings out the best in us.

As the region struggled, individuals and businesses came forth as never before. Residents of high-rise buildings helped those who could not navigate ten and twenty flights of stairs in the dark; businesses and customers alike helped badly damaged businesses; money and supplies came pouring into the region. Many businesses provided vital services for other businesses. Salvage Data, for example, offered free hard drive recovery evaluations, insurance documentation support, and free storage for recovered data. Even the Occupy Wall Street movement quickly organized to become Recovery.org.

Fannie Mae and Freddie Mac, the giant institutions that own or guarantee large numbers of home mortgages, announced they were suspending mortgage payment obligations for ninety days.

Donations poured in from businesses. But it was not all about money. Verizon Wireless stores let people come in and charge their mobile phones, use Wi-Fi, and make free domestic calls. AT&T rolled out charging vans. Duracell ran mobile charging stations and gave out free batteries. Chevrolet donated dozens of vans and other vehicles to help the Red Cross in its rescue effort. U-Haul provided free business storage for thirty days.

Office Depot Foundation funded the U.S. Chamber's Business Civic Leadership Center help desk, fielding recovery questions from small businesses, and taking pledges from businesses large and small. The Manhattan Chamber of Commerce created a Small Business Recovery Fund to accept donations for microgrants to help small businesses meet immediate expenses.

What People Said

If one were to write a report card on how the region fared in response to the storm, a fair score would be in the mid to high 80s. The examples of leadership, resilience, and people and businesses helping each other could fill volumes. Pulling the score down were pockets of tough issues, including a much-criticized electric utility serving Long Island, and claims of recovery help too little too late in Staten Island and other areas.

Three weeks after the storm, Quinnipiac University conducted a survey of 1,165 New York City residents.

New York City voters said overwhelmingly that Gov. Andrew Cuomo and Mayor Michael Bloomberg did an "excellent" or "good" job responding to Hurricane Sandy. The best marks in the region went to New Jersey Governor Chris Christie and President Barack Obama.

A total of 86 percent of New York City voters said the overall storm response from first responders was "excellent" or "good." Grades for other organizations:

- Utility companies: 37 percent "excellent" or "good," with 58 percent "not so good" or "poor"
- Metropolitan Transportation Authority: 75 percent "excellent" or "good"
- Red Cross: 66 percent "excellent" or "good"

Next time?

"If the preventive measures cost billions," New Yorkers say, "let's spend it."

Leadership

For those in the region who were able to watch the succession of TV press conferences, hear them on radio, or get the highlights on tweets or text messages, it was clear that the respective governors and mayors were working long and hard to support the rescue and recovery. New Jersey Governor Christie differed in style from New York City Mayor Michael Bloomberg, as did President Obama and all the others. What they shared in common were a number of very important communications characteristics. They:

- Communicated frequently.
- Provided specific information. The news was tough, sometimes necessarily lacking answers (as in when power would come back to specific areas), and it was blunt. People in crisis situations, research has found, want to hear the good news as well as the bad. And that was what they delivered.

The subjective quality of leadership came through, proving that the leaders were in charge, and were able to rally that feeling that we will come though this. It will not be easy, but we will do it. As FDR said in his 1933 inaugural, when the nation faced the Depression, "We have nothing to fear but fear itself."

Lessons Learned

Crisis plans for homes and businesses help in dozens of ways. Ready.gov, the Department of Homeland Security website, has good guidance for homes and businesses who do not already have plans.

Business continuity plans are another vital planning resource. Who does what and how when a business cannot open requires complex planning and testing. It is this latter phase, the testing, that is especially critical. You don't want to activate an untested plan.

Another lesson was the need to have backups for key personnel, and backups for critical information now stored on iPhones and other devices. Paper is the answer when all else fails.

Commercial buildings in the path of the surging water—e.g., in the Lower Manhattan-Wall Street area—should not wait for new regulations on placement of HVAC and other infrastructure. If the equipment is in the basement, it should be moved to higher floors.

Amid all the bad news—and there was lots of it—a striking story of prevention is worth noting, as reported in the *New York Times* on December 3, 2012 ("Resisted For Blocking the View, Dunes Prove They Blunt Storms"):

"[S]ix years ago, after the Army Corps of Engineers proposed to erect dunes and elevate beaches along more than six miles of coast to protect the barrier island, the Long Beach City Council vetoed 5 to 0 its $7 million initial share and (proposal for) taking part . . . Point Lookout, Lido Beach, and Atlantic Beach approved construction of fifteen-foot-high dunes as storm insurance. Those dunes did their job, sparing them catastrophic damage while Long Beach suffered at least $200 million in property and infrastructure losses, according to preliminary estimates."

Less than a year after Hurricane Sandy, a presidential task force whose purpose it was to assess lessons learned from Sandy, urged communities to plan to shore up buildings and power grids – a harsh reality of rising sea levels and climate change.

Prevention—Comparing Very Different Crises

BP and the Deepwater Horizon Oil Spill

In 2010, the largest oil spill on record began with an underwater explosion, causing the deep well to gush oil for three months, until the well was capped. As a series of trial-and-error methods were employed to seal the source, fifty-three thousand barrels of crude oil spilled into the Gulf of

Mexico each day. Tar balls and oil sheens gave but a hint of the damage to beaches and fishing industries in the area.

A January 2011 White House report put the blame for the spill squarely on BP and its vendors, Transocean and Halliburton, for a series of cost-cutting measures and lack of proper safety efforts. BP has admitted to negligence and will pay billions in fines and help to restore the region.

As the efforts were under way to contain the spill, BP's CEO, Tony Hayward, as spokesperson for the vast media coverage, became yet another example of an insensitive spokesperson. He never connected to the audience on an empathy level, and angered affected residents of the area as he was seen vacationing far from the Gulf of Mexico. During an interview, presumably alluding to the time the capping of the well was taking, he said that "[he] wanted [his] life back" He no longer is chairman and CEO of BP.

The Madoff Scandal

Bernard Madoff, a trusted investment manager and former chairman of NASDAQ, confessed in December 2008 that his business was an elaborate Ponzi scheme.

A Ponzi scheme is an investment fraud that involves the payment of purported returns to existing investors from funds contributed by new investors, though investors are not told that this is occurring. Ponzi scheme organizers often solicit new investors by deceptively promising to invest funds in opportunities claimed to generate high returns with little or no risk. The schemes are named after Charles Ponzi, who duped thousands of New England residents into investing in a postage stamp speculation in the 1920s, at a time when annual bank account interest rates were 5 percent. He promised investors he could provide a 50-percent return in just ninety days.

Despite the illusion of growth and safe investment, Madoff's nearly five thousand clients were left with virtually no assets, a loss estimated in the billions. Unlike the promises of many Ponzi schemes, he did not promote spectacular short-term returns. Instead, investors' account statements showed consistently moderate, returns, even during turbulent market conditions. Nonetheless, they were false.

The morning after the news broke, National Public Radio ran an interview with one of his clients. She recalled her trust in him but now reflected that, if only she had questioned his monthly statements (which she admitted she did not understand), perhaps she could have ceased doing business with him and been spared her loss.

Madoff is now serving a 150-year prison sentence, as investigators continue to determine others involved in the case and recover as many assets as they can for the former Madoff clients.

There is the tale of the Madoff whistleblower.

Harry M. Markopolos, a former securities industry investigator and independent financial fraud investigator, says that the blame lies at the doors of the Securities and Exchange Commission for ignoring repeated tips that could have led to an early discovery and avoidance of the crisis.

In 1999—nearly ten years before the Madoff confession and meltdown of the entire assets were revealed—Markopolos and some colleagues examined the public filings at the SEC and determined that there was no way these investments were making the money that Madoff claimed. In 2000 Markopolos filed a complaint with the Boston office of the SEC. No action was taken, and he filed a more detailed complaint a year later. This too led to no action. Driven by an intellectual challenge, he deepened his analysis and investigation,

By November 2005, in a filing to the SEC, he said:

"Bernie Madoff is running the world's largest unregistered hedge fund."

In Congressional testimony and on *60 Minutes*, Markopolos continued his march, declaring: "Nothing was done. There was an abject failure by the regulatory agencies we entrust as our watchdog."

While the story has more twists and turns and tales of misdirected trust, the fact is that a whistleblower had the real story early and was ignored. There were a number of missteps. When Markopolos reported the irregularities to the Boston office of the SEC, staff members did nothing simply because it was not in their jurisdiction, since the Madoff business was in New York City.

Whistleblowers by their nature rock the boat. They may be insistent and unrelenting. Though they can, as in this case, hold the fabric of truth,they need to have a good grasp of the system; and it takes open-minded bureaucrats to listen. They did not until it was way too late.

The Sinking of the *Costa Concordia*

On a clear night in January 2012, the *Costa Concordia*, one of the most modern cruise ships afloat, capsized and sank off the coast of the tiny Italian island of Giglio. Thirty two people died of the total 4,252 guests aboard.

The sinking rocked the cruise industry, which is generally known for safety. I have been, for professional and vacation reasons, on several dozen cruise ships, and have never seen a problem. Except for occasional rough weather and rocking and rolling at times, a cruise ship feels safe and is safe.

On the January night off the coast of the Italian island, however, the ship, cruising unusually close to land, hit rocks and took on water through a large gash in the hull. Had the captain acted quickly to evacuate the ship, everyone on board would have been safe. Instead, for reasons that have never been clear, he at first denied a problem, simply announcing a temporary electrical problem. As the water-saturated ship began to tilt perilously, the "abandon ship" announcement came, but the ship had already tilted to such a degree that most of lifeboats on the side facing inward toward the water were useless. It was far too late to avert chaos and some loss of life.

This is not only a case of a captain who ignored all the rules of safety at sea as the ship took on water. It also is an example of the Italian-based management of Costa Cruises (a division of Carnival Corporation) turning its back on the risky practice of what is called "touristic approaches," an odd effort to bring a ship close to shore, presumably so that the residents of the island could glimpse this huge ship close up. When Costa ships had done so in the past, they were lucky. This time they were not.

Earlier Examples at Sea

The Sinking of the *Titanic*

The RMS *Titanic*, considered unsinkable, sailed under loose international laws governing the number of lifeboats on a ship. In 1912, the *Titanic* sailed with only twenty lifeboats capable of carrying 1,178 people for the 2,223 passengers and 899 crew members on board. Had there been enough seats for everyone, many more would have survived. In the years that followed, international regulations were strengthened considerably, and today's passenger and cruise ships follow very strict guidelines for adequate lifeboat capacity for passengers and crew.

The lifeboat issue aside, the calamity could have been avoided, The captain had received several radio warnings from other ships to watch for ice in the North Atlantic, and the crow's nest did watch for the ice, though the seamen on the lookout did not have binoculars (a curious lapse that has never been explained). By the time the huge, black ice formation was spotted, and despite quick attempts to reverse the ship's engines, it was too late.

In 1912, long before today's mass media coverage of Senate hearings, the *Titanic* hearing was a major occasion, lasting seventeen days. Here are excerpts:

Senator William Alden Smith: Suppose you had glasses [binoculars] . . . could you have seen this black object [the iceberg] at a greater distance?

Lookout Frederick Fleet: We could have seen it a bit sooner.

Smith: How much sooner?

Fleet: Well, enough to get out of the way.

J. Bruce Ismay, president of the White Star Line, the British owner of the *Titanic*, also testified, speaking here about his experience after jumping into a lifeboat fairly early in the crisis:

Smith: You did not see her go down?

Ismay: No, sir.

Smith: How far were you from the ship?

Ismay: I do not know how far we were away. I was sitting with my back to the ship. I was rowing all the time I was in the boat. We were pulling away.

Smith: You did not see her go down?

Ismay: I am glad I did not.

("Word for Word: The *Titanic* Disaster," *New York Times*, Dec. 28, 1997)

After:

Additional boats were immediately installed on North Atlantic ships. And within a year, international regulations required muster drills and lifeboats for everyone.

Terrorists Hijack the *S.S. Achille Lauro*

In October 1985, four members of the Palestine Liberation Front held the passengers of the cruise chip Achille Lauro hostage off the Egyptian coast, demanding that Israel release fifty Palestinian prisoners. Wielding weapons they had brought on board, they shot wheelchair-bound American passenger Leon Klinghoffer and threw his body overboard. The hijackers, boarding the ship with the other passengers, had slipped on board without so much as an inspection, which might have revealed their weapons.

After:
Like the sinking of the *Titanic*, this incident led to maritime reforms—this time an overhaul of security practices aboard passenger vessels.

Challenges on Today's Oceans

The rapidly growing cruise industry had immediate reasons to tighten security after 9/11, given the concerns of the traveling public. With bigger ships on order, some carrying more than four thousand guests and one thousand-plus crew members, everyone needed assurances. Royal Caribbean Cruises' leadership, along with others in the industry, moved faster than any other business in the United States to tighten access to the ships, with photos embedded in what is known as the SeaPass Card. Security staffing was increased, and every item coming on board at any time—whether luggage or supplies—is subjected to X-ray screening or other means, including highly trained canines.

Cargo ship screening—admittedly a more complex challenge—continues to be debated among shippers and port security officials. Some form of technology will doubtless be the answer, but decisions could be a long way off.

And finally, port security, specifically for authorization of people entering for business reasons, continues to be inconsistent, with a checkerboard of procedures. The guards at the gates at many ports continue to be among the lowest-level security available, and some often do not even know whom they work for.

The Safety Issue—A Quick Look Back

The Triangle Shirtwaist Fire

On a Saturday afternoon in 1911, the Triangle Shirtwaist Company factory on the eighth, ninth, and tenth floors of a "fireproof" building off Washington Square in New York City became the scene of a massive tragedy in which 141 young men and women factory workers perished, unable to escape the flames and smoke from a fire that erupted among highly flammable fabrics. Many escaped down the stairs before the fire spread; others were cut off by flames and, seeing no other way out, jumped to their deaths. No one except the factory's owners, who escaped, knew of the way to safety through the roof.

The Triangle Shirtwaist fire illustrated a fact well known to New York City garment workers at that time—that most garment factories were potential firetraps, with bins of highly flammable textiles and patterns surrounded by smoking workers and overworked sewing machines that sometimes overheated and caused small fires. In fact, the Triangle Shirtwaist Company had already been cited for fire safety concerns.

After:

The incident led to a number of reforms—but not before the insensitive local Manufacturers' Association called a meeting to find ways to avoid the reforms to protect workers.

The Triangle Shirtwaist fire of 1911 would change the way government regulated worker safety. Before the fire, government had mostly stayed away from businesses, feeling it had no authority to regulate them. The Triangle Shirtwaist fire remains as a turning point in U.S. history. Countless state and federal laws were enacted because of this incident, and unions gained numerous new workers who wanted someone to fight for their safety.

In a more perfect world, with more fire safety regulations, more people would have escaped from the World Trade Center on 9/11, ninety years later.

To Recall or Not to Recall?

Tylenol: The Big Wake-Up Call

The 1982 Tylenol tampering crisis marked the birth of modern-day crisis management. Johnson & Johnson's handling of the crime against innocent consumers and against the Tylenol brand established solid criteria:

- Be quick to respond.
- Show you care about the public.
- Do something about the problem.
- Explain it all through regular contact with the media.

Throughout the crisis, J&J's CEO, Jim Burke, showed how to be direct and caring, and that a corporation can show a strong and compassionate face.

The Tylenol Tampering and the Birth of
Twentieth-Century Crisis Management

"Cases of full disclosure in business abound, but Johnson & Johnson probably set the gold standard with its handling of the Tylenol crisis in the 1980s."
—*Jack Welch and Suzy Welch,* Winning

In 1982, seven people in the Chicago area died after taking Tylenol (a product of Johnson's McNeil Pharmaceutical division) that had been laced with cyanide. Until then, product tampering was a rare event in a world of easy-to-open bottles and packages. These poisonings remain an unsolved mystery.

Johnson & Johnson's handling of the Tylenol tampering may be remembered most for J&J chairman Jim Burke's quick decision to protect the public by recalling the entire supply of Tylenol from the nation's retail shelves; communicating openly with the public; and, in less than three months, introducing a newly formed product in tamper-proof packaging. By any stretch, this was a difficult decision, given the product's 35 percent share of the $1 billion analgesic market—and the fact that Tylenol contributed about 20 percent of J&J's profits.

In the midst of the crisis, J&J commissioned substantial opinion polling and found that 87 percent of the public realized J&J was not responsible for the murders, though 61 percent said they were not likely to buy extra-strength capsules again. Tylenol did rebound. And company morale soared.

On February 10, 1986, history repeated itself when J&J and the Food and Drug Administration again received a report of a death linked to the lacing of Tylenol capsules with cyanide.

The management of the landmark Tylenol tampering crisis was not merely about a compassionate and effective communication program. The reintroduction of Tylenol in tamper-proof packaging heralded the beginning of tamper-proof packaging for nearly every food, drug, and small consumer package found on store shelves today.

Robert Kniffen, J&J's vice president of corporate relations at the time, commented on the decision process and the J&J Credo:

"I was in the president's office at McNeil Consumer and he had asked the vice president of finance to compute what it would cost to recall all of the capsules in the United States. This guy came back and said he calculated that it would be seventy-five million dollars. And then he said, 'but we don't have seventy-five million dollars.' Then there was a pause and another guy said, 'But how can we not do this, because there might be another bottle on the shelf, and if we don't get them back, someone might die.' It was not an instance when someone said, 'Let's consult the Credo and think through this problem, starting with our responsibility to the consumer,' but rather it was a way of looking at the world, at business, and at the decisions. The Credo structures the way you think about things. When all that was done and the dust had settled, we reached the conclusion that those hundreds of individual decisions were right decisions. They sprang from some common way of looking at the world, which in retrospect was the Credo.

"I was convinced we were going to lose the brand," continued Kniffen. "As the result of that (the recall), we did find three bottles on the shelves in Chicago that were poisoned."

(Patricia Jones and Larry Kahaner,
Say It and Live It, Doubleday, 1985)

Burke commented at the time: "After the crisis was over, we realized that no meeting had been called to make the first critical decision. Every one of us knew what we had to do. We had the Credo to guide us." Kniffen explains, "At Johnson & Johnson there is no mission statement that hangs on the wall. Instead, for more than sixty years, a simple, one-page document—our Credo—has guided our actions in fulfilling our responsibilities to our customers, our employees, the community, and our stockholders. Our worldwide family of companies shares this value system in thirty-six languages spreading across Africa, Asia/Pacific, Eastern Europe, Europe, Latin America, the Middle East, and North America." (Patricia Jones and Larry Kahaner, *Say It and Live It*)

Below is that document:

Our Credo

We believe our first responsibility is to the doctors, nurses, and patients, to mothers and fathers and all others who use our products and services.

In meeting their needs everything we do must be of high quality.

We must constantly strive to reduce our costs in order to maintain reasonable prices.

Customers' orders must be serviced promptly and accurately.

Our suppliers and distributors must have an opportunity to make a fair profit.

We are responsible to our employees, the men and women who work with us throughout the world.

Everyone must be considered as an individual.

We must respect their dignity and recognize their merit.

They must have a sense of security in their jobs.

Compensation must be fair and adequate, and working conditions clean, orderly, and safe.

We must be mindful of ways to help our employees fulfill their family responsibilities.

Employees must feel free to make suggestions and complaints.

There must be equal opportunity for employment, development, and advancement for those qualified.

We must provide competent management, and their actions must be just and ethical.

We are responsible to the communities in which we live and work and to the world community as well.

We must be good citizens—support good works and charities and bear our fair share of taxes.

We must encourage civic improvements and better health and education.

We must maintain in good order the property we are privileged to use, protecting the environment and natural resources.

Our final responsibility is to our stockholders.

Business must make a sound profit.

We must experiment with new ideas.

Research must be carried on, innovative programs developed, and mistakes paid for.

New equipment must be purchased, new facilities provided, and new products launched.

Reserves must be created to provide for adverse times.

When we operate according to these principles, the stockholders should realize a fair return.

Jim Collins, author of *Good to Great*, talks about an event that occurred three years before the Tylenol tampering, when Burke ". . . pulled twenty key executives into a room and thumped his finger on a copy of the J&J Credo. Penned thirty-six years earlier by R.W. Johnson Jr., it laid out the 'We hold these truths to be self-evident' of the Johnson & Johnson Co., among them a higher duty to 'mothers and all others that use our products.' Burke worried that executives had come to view the Credo as an artifact. . . . 'I said, "Here's the Credo. If we're not going to live by it, let's tear it off the wall." Burke later told Joseph Badaracco and Richard Ellsworth for their book, *Leadership and The Quest for Integrity*, '[T]he room erupted into a debate that ended with recommitment. Burke and his colleagues would conduct similar meetings around the world, reviving the Credo as a living document.' " (Jim Collins, "What These Extraordinary Leaders Can Teach Today's Troubled Executives," *Fortune*, July 21, 2003)

At the November 1982 press conference reintroducing Tylenol, Jim Burke said:

"It is our job at Johnson & Johnson to ensure the survival of Tylenol, and we are pledged to do this. While we consider this crime an assault on society, we are nevertheless ready to fulfill our responsibility, which includes paying the price of this heinous crime. But I urge you not to make Tylenol the scapegoat.

"I am confident that the news media, working in its own way and according to its own dictates, will help us to dispel these fears about a product that rightfully earned the confidence of the public. We welcome any help we can get from you and others in the vast rebuilding task that lies ahead."

After:

The Food and Drug Administration enacted regulations requiring that over-the-counter drugs and certain medical devices and cosmetic products be marketed in tamper-resistant packages. Second, Congress enacted the Federal Anti-Tampering Act, which gives authority to the FDA, the U.S. Department of Agriculture and the FBI to follow up on tampering violations, requiring penalties, including fines and imprisonment, for tampering or falsely reporting tampering.

I am often asked about what all of this meant and how it came to spawn an entire public affairs specialty. While the advice to be open, candid, decisive, and responsive to the public was sound, the real credit for the successful handling of the crisis goes to Jim Burke. The solid advice he received validated not only his best instincts but also the strength of the company's corporate Credo. Through the simplicity of his messages, empathy for every customer, and the decisive action to recall the product, Burke was able to transcend the stereotype of the monolithic, anonymous corporation, and limit the damage to the brand.

Andy Gilman, CEO of CommCore Consulting Group, coached Jim Burke for his countless media appearances during the crisis. He shared some of his thoughts:

"My initial impressions were that he was a no-nonsense CEO. But he was also one of the few CEOs I met who was passionately concerned with the customers. Many have learned how to say the appropriate words of concern; I got the sense that Burke was serious about this. I recall one prep session for the national satellite press conference to announce the return of Tylenol to the shelves. Burke gave an answer to a question according to the prepared Q&A. It was adequate, but he didn't feel the answer was good enough for the public. He said, 'I need more information that will help customers before I answer that.' The question that John Stossel asked him during one of the *20/20* interviews typified Burke's attitude. Stossel played a tape in which Burke choked up as he announced the death of one of the victims of the poisonings. Burke then went on to talk about some business and customer plans. The quote I believe from Stossel was that 'you mix decency with cunning . . .'" (Interview by author)

J&J's famous Credo meant something. There was a values system in place. The company also had deposits of goodwill in its PR bank.

The managers did make smart decisions. They pulled a strong team together and worked on it. They went above and beyond what they had to do. The government at first did not require tamper-proof packaging, and certainly not triplicate seals.

The Credo was not discussed in every meeting, but its philosophy permeated their thinking. It's similar to a code of ethics; once it's been taught to a group, family, or society, they make decisions with this embedded in their thought process. One of the ethical questions: "Is this the right thing to do?"

The FDA has noticed that when one tampering occurs, a number of other incidents generally occur in rapid succession. In the months and years that followed, the FDA was involved in a widespread series of investigations that included dozens of products, most notably Gerber baby food, Girl Scout cookies, and more over-the-counter drugs. This suggests a pattern of "copycat" tamperings, which could be attributed to a desire by some consumers for either attention or the quick settlement of fraudulent monetary claims. Whether these are false alarms or petty legal claims, they occasionally create increasing pressures on companies.

Pepsi and the Needle Hoax

Several years after the Tylenol episodes, a Tacoma, Washington, man claimed he had found a syringe in a can of Diet Pepsi. A media frenzy began as several similar claims were made. Pepsi management and the FDA, perplexed by the claims, conducted thorough searches and investigations, which showed that such claims were impossible. Pepsi even proved it by showing the details of the canning process on TV news programs across the nation.

As Dr. David Kessler, FDA commissioner, said at the time, "You never say never, and certainly we are inspecting. But tampering would certainly be difficult to do." (Martin Tolchin, "U.S. Official Has Doubts About Pepsi Tampering," *New York Times*, June 17, 1993)

After nearly a week of headlines and more copycat claims, an in-store surveillance camera showed a customer boldly slipping a syringe into a Diet Pepsi can. FDA Commissioner Kessler then officially ended the crisis by declaring it was a hoax.

Pepsi's frequent and clear communications to the public were reminiscent of the Tylenol crisis—and, interestingly, were driven in large measure by Pepsi's corporate credo, which states that customer safety comes first and that communication should be fast and open.

Throughout the week, Pepsi stood firm in its decision not to issue a recall order—believing that to have done so would have given the criminals more satisfaction. Had there been any deaths, the recall decision would likely have been different. The stock price held firm throughout the week.

Each day, from the start, Pepsi conducted a survey of 150 consumers. When asked to react to the statement, "I feel the Pepsi-Cola Company is handling the issue in a responsible manner," the responses averaged an 85 percent affirmation. ("The Pepsi Hoax: What Went Wrong," The Pepsi-Cola Company, 1993)

Looking at the consumers-turned-criminals behind this crisis, Stanton Samenow, author of *Inside the Criminal Mind*, referred to those who tamper with cans or make copycat claims. "It's absolute personal glorification and satisfaction when he or she sits back and watches an entire nation react just baffled. It's a feeling of power and control; he has outsmarted the nation. Everyone is talking about it." ("For Copycats, 'A Feeling of Power, Control,' " *USA Today*, June 17, 1993)

Glass in Gerber Baby Food

Following a report that a mother in New York had found pieces of glass in a jar of Gerber baby food, Gerber was faced with the tough decisions all consumer product companies face when they get news of this sort. Do we recall the product? And if not, what do we do?

Gerber, like Pepsi, stood fast and did not issue a recall, but did an exhaustive investigation of the batch in question and found no glass. Copycat reports flowed in, and Gerber checked on every one. Nonetheless, public confidence and market share dropped, but were restored to nearly their original levels after a vigorous public relations and marketing program—which included tours of the plants for reporters, a mailing to 2.6 million households showing the proper way to open a jar, and an ongoing communication program to employees, doctors, trade customers, and government authorities.

Benzene in Perrier

Perrier, long considered the icon of bottled water, shocked the U.S. public in 1990 when North Carolina health officials discovered low levels of benzene in the water. Benzene is a carcinogen. The company first responded that this was an isolated incident caused by an operator error at one plant. When it soon was learned that the benzene was in the product in Europe as well, an angry public forced a worldwide recall of Perrier—an immediate blow to its market share as other bottled waters took their place in bars and on grocery shelves.

Coca-Cola

Another beverage icon, Coca-Cola, withdrew 15 million cans of various soft drinks in Belgium when consumers reported a number of problems, including the hospitalization of forty students with symptoms of food poisoning.

A series of events overwhelmed the company—including the carbon dioxide in the soda being tainted with sulfur, and a fungicide attaching itself to the bottoms of cans. The European offices did not notify the corporation's Atlanta headquarters of the problems until three days after the emergencies. Had Atlanta been notified immediately, as good practice dictates, Atlanta might have asked the right questions and supported the European operations—avoiding denials which led to headlines and loss of faith in Coke.

By 2002, product recalls for a variety reasons—from defects to tamperings—had risen so much that the public was ignoring a good many of them.

Recalls—Lessons Learned

When the dust from the Tylenol tamperings had settled, public affairs professionals and many companies renewed their efforts to understand how crises arise and how responses should be fashioned. What we concluded was that crisis management follows a pattern:

• The pre-crisis stage: Companies begin to identify potential risks or problems, develop crisis plans, and conduct simulations and training to prepare employees to handle crises, and take steps to prevent some crises from even happening.

• The crisis stage (if one occurs): Companies, guided by their crisis plans, assess the situation, begin to investigate the cause(s) of the crisis, take actions to end it, and communicate this information to a host of stakeholders. The role of the CEO is especially important in this stage, and the Tylenol legacy has a lasting effect by identifying Jim Burke as the role model for the spokesperson under fire—calm, compassionate, decisive, and out front.

• The post-crisis or recovery stage: Repair possible damage to brand reputation, share price, and corporate reputation.

Air Florida

Consider the Air Florida crash of 1982, where seventy-nine passengers perished in a crash into the icy Potomac River shortly after takeoff in a blinding snowstorm. The wings, it turned out, were heavily weighed down by ice and the plane crashed on takeoff.

After:
De-icing practices and regulations now are standard.

Exxon Valdez

The *Exxon Valdez* oil spill of nearly eleven million gallons of crude oil became an icon of how not to respond to a crisis. Interestingly, the Valdez spill was not one of the biggest (though any spill is serious), but it is remembered in the hall of fame of oil spills because of lack of response and lack of caring. For hours and days of silence, Exxon CEO Lawrence Rawl was conspicuous for his absence and lack of public statements of concern. It was rumored that Rawl was suspicious of the media and this affected his decision to avoid the spotlight. Some sources even reported that requests for interviews were met with replies that Rawl had no time for that sort of thing.

After about a week, Frank Iarossi, who ran Exxon Shipping, held a press conference in Valdez, delivering what he thought was some good news about the cleanup—and was immediately contradicted by the media and

local fishermen. Amid the communications delays, Iarossi announced that
the cleanup was under way, when in fact the only action that had taken place
to that point was a boat tour of the area to assess the damage.

When Rawl finally did face the media, it was on live television.
When asked about the plans for the cleanup, it was clear he had not read
the plans, and stated it was not the job of the chairman to read reports of
this type.

While the ship's captain was found to have been intoxicated,
Exxon's CEO finally did visit the site—after more than two weeks. Some
consumer boycotts linger to this day. Fines and cleanup costs eventually cost
the company billions.

Exxon's CEO and senior management, perceived as being aloof and
underestimating the problem, suffered lingering criticism remembered
more than twenty-five years later.

Though the bulk of the actual blame for the accident has
appropriately fallen on the shoulders of the ship's captain, Ed Hazelwood,
investigations have also shown that company-mandated cuts in the size of
tanker crews could have been a contributing factor—or at the least could
have helped to prevent the accident had the cuts not been enforced. In such
situations, smaller crews are overworked and are more prone to fatigue.

On the night of the accident, a local pilot, as is customary, guided
the boat out of the port. Hazelwood then left the bridge and went to his
cabin. Records show that his departure from the bridge before the ship
reached the open ocean was a violation. Add to that another violation: The
third mate he assigned to the bridge was not licensed to steer the ship in
the coastal waters.

But looking at Hazelwood himself, it was well known on the tanker
and in the company that he had an alcohol abuse history. This was especially
ironic, as he also was known as the best captain in the company's fleet.

After:
• Stiffer government regulations and increased spill-prevention
requirements and response procedures by Alyeska Pipeline Service, the
industry consortium that manages the Valdez port terminal and the eight-
hundred-mile Trans-Alaska Pipeline, are in place.
• Oil industry safety standards have been tightened, along with
emergency response planning.
• Escort tugs now accompany outbound tankers.

• The U.S. Coast Guard has increased tracking procedures.
• Ship captains are tested for alcohol and drugs.
• The biggest risk reduction comes from the requirement—mandatory by 2015—that oil tankers must be constructed as double hull vessels, so that should an accident occur and the outer hull is damaged, the oil would be retained behind the second wall.

And Exxon Valdez is now part of the lexicon of how not to handle a crisis, especially with regard to corporate arrogance and how not to communicate.

False Alarms

An entire book could be devoted to the false alarms and scares of the past few decades. The media and the public have jumped on a number of health-related scares that, after careful analysis, were empty. The Alar scare of 1989 showed how one TV program, *60 Minutes*, could bring the entire apple industry to near ruin when the program reported that the chemical preservative used on apples could cause cancer in children.

Or consider the Harvard research that claimed that two cups of coffee a day doubled the risk of pancreatic cancer, and three cups nearly tripled it. Five years later, the same Harvard group repeated the study and failed to confirm the findings. (Jane Brody, "Health Scares that Weren't So Scary," *New York Times*, August 18, 1998)

The Alar Scare

The Natural Resources Defense Council organized a public relations campaign claiming that Alar, a chemical sprayed on apples so that they would ripen with some consistency, would cause cancer, and the media responded vigorously. Apples, the American fruit icon, were now forbidden fruit. It was *60 Minutes* that led the pack, with the news that this chemical was a human carcinogen. Public outcry following the media reports forced growers to stop using Alar, and the chemical's manufacturer, Uniroyal, pulled it from the market. And the apple industry was left in shambles.

Subsequent tests by the National Cancer Institute and the Environmental Protection Agency showed no cancer connection. The reality was, according to the International Apple Institute, if there were any threat at all, one would have to eat twenty-eight thousand apples a day for a lifetime.

Deny the Problem and the Customers Will Force Change

Intel

In 1994, Intel learned that when a customer is concerned, it is time to pay attention and not minimize the problem. The problem in this case was a flaw in a chip used for mathematical calculating that had the potential for a rare miscalculation—again, a case where the consumer does not want to be or cannot afford to be the one with the failing chip. Intel at first minimized the problem, initially brought to its attention when Thomas Nicely, a mathematician at Lynchburg College in Virginia, posted a note to a website describing how his processor had erred in dividing two fractions. Reports of miscalculations then flowed in through the website, while Intel turned its back on the consumer concerns.

Months of public criticism of Intel came to a climax when giant customer IBM canceled orders for the chips and accused Intel of underestimating the potential for error. After months of increasingly bad publicity, Intel apologized to all customers and offered replacement chips. According to The Wall Street Journal: "Investors reacted favorably to Intel's move, sending the company's stock, which had plummeted after the IBM announcement, up $3.4375 to $61.25 a share. . . . Analysts said the increase reflected a belief that the episode was now behind Intel, and that it won't badly hurt Intel's earnings or fundamental market position." (Jim Carlton and Stephen Kerider Yoder, "Humble Pie: Intel to Replace its Pentium Chips," *Wall Street Journal*, December 21, 1994)

In an interview with the *Wall Street Journal*, Intel CEO Andy Grove said: "To some people this seemed arrogant and uncaring. We apologize for that. Intel's old replacement policy was based on an 'Intel-knows-best' attitude. . . . We came to the realization that what upset people was, here was Intel making decisions for them." ("Firm Reverses Itself on Pentium Policy," *Wall Street Journal*, December 21, 1994)

Grove, reflecting in his memoirs: "[M]ost CEOs are in the center of a fortified palace, and news from the outside has to percolate through layers of people from the periphery where the action is . . . it took a barrage of relentless criticism to make me realize that something had changed. . . . We need to expose ourselves to our customers. . . . We need to expose ourselves to lower-level employees who, when encouraged, will tell us a lot that we need to know. We must invite comments even from people whose job it is to constantly evaluate and criticize us, such as journalists and members of the financial community; as we throw ourselves into raw action, our senses and instincts will rapidly be honed again." (Andrew S. Grove, *Only the Paranoid Survive*, Currency, 1996, reported in "How We Miscalculated," *Time*, September 2, 1996)

Bureaucracy and Bureaucrats

The Chicago Flood of 1992

An ordinary bureaucratic order to immediately repair a crack in a tunnel under the Chicago River turned into a flood and chaos for downtown Chicago when a city worker ignored the order. The bureaucrat, instead of heeding the urgency of the situation—at a repair cost of approximately $10,000—took the time to get competitive estimates as the crack widened and the tunnel flooded. The acting transportation commissioner was fired, but too late to prevent the huge floods that closed two hundred office buildings, knee-deep in water and without power, for days.

Stanford University

After several attempts to be considered for an entry-level accounting position at Stanford were ignored, an accountant finally found a position with the U.S. government. By coincidence, he was assigned to audit Stanford's government research grants. He found a pattern of unauthorized charges for such items as flowers for the university president's wedding reception and furniture for his home.

While the university quickly hired an independent auditing firm to investigate, correct the problem, and install new accounting safeguards, Stanford President Donald Kennedy refused to be contrite, especially when facing a congressional subcommittee. Shortly after his embarrassing testimony, the Stanford board of trustees asked for his resignation.

Corporate Shenanigans

Unprecedented financial scandals that harmed helpless shareholders and employees were topped by the collapse of Enron and its auditor, Arthur Andersen. Tyco and WorldCom competed for the headlines as well, all with a common thread: financial hubris, where the senior executives thought they would not be caught. They were caught, and joined their fellow CEOs in jail.

Enron, WorldCom, Tyco, Qwest, and Global Crossing—a few of the more startling financial failures of recent years—destroyed a combined $460 billion in shareholder value.

Hewlett-Packard

And along comes HP, newly refocused and rolling along after the demise of controversial CEO Carly Fiorina—with news that the company's chair, Patricia Dunn, was accused of directing or at least sanctioning investigations of board members who allegedly leaked news to the media. The roots of the problem go back to the highly controversial acquisition of Compaq, a lagging computer maker seen by Fiorina as the future of HP. The board battle, played out in headlines, sowed the seeds for a divided board.

As news of board problems leaked, the company hired private detectives to trail board members and even a star reporter for the *Wall Street Journal*. After an agonizing public display of scrutiny, Dunn was declared innocent at last—though she no longer is board chair.

A.H. Robins & the Dalkon Shield

A.H. Robins Company, makers of the Dalkon Shield intrauterine birth control device (and a number of famous consumer products such as Robitussin and ChapStick) faced a consumer class action suit claiming that the Dalkon product had caused a number of injuries and deaths. Although the product had been taken off the market years before the class action suit, the litigation revealed that the company had relied on inadequate safety tests and had ignored safety warnings from the product's inventor. The company CEO, fearing the pressure of the media, did not respond to interviews.

Faced with a mountain of lawsuits, the company filed for bankruptcy and eventually sold its famous brands.

Enron and Arthur Andersen Go Down in Flames

Massive energy trader Enron shocked the world with its collapse, falling like dominoes. "Enron's fatal flaw," according to *Time* magazine, "was management hubris, tacitly encouraged by board members, regulators, politicians, and stock analysts—many with financial ties to Enron—who looked the other way as warning lights began to flash. Feeling it could do no wrong, the company too often pursued unprofitable markets, obscured the costs, and stiff-armed anyone who asked for an explanation." (Daniel Kadlec, "Power Failure," *Time*, December 10, 2001)

Within a year of the breaking news, the company's stock lost 99 percent of its value. Innocent shareholders, including thousands of employees, lost billions.

The failures were compounded by evidence that Enron's auditor, the once-venerable Arthur Andersen accounting firm, had instructed staff members to destroy Enron audit materials, thus obstructing the government's investigation of fraud at Enron—making it very difficult to untangle the web of Enron's creation of partnerships with shell companies, the creation of which made many Enron executives rich. The scandal brought Arthur Andersen to an untimely grave as well.

Tyco International

In the golden days of Dennis Kozlowski, a visit to Tyco International's headquarters on Manhattan's 57th Street was more like visiting a museum of antiquities. Perched on a high floor, with sweeping views of Central Park, Tyco's offices bore no evidence of its diverse businesses or any credo. Antique rugs, precious Old World oil paintings, and the resident chef and wandering shoeshine lady gave the impression of a fine way of life at Tyco.

Kozlowski commuted between the company's modest New Hampshire office, the sunny high rise in Boca Raton, Florida, and his yacht *Endeavor* and New York City headquarters. At its most frantic pace of acquisitions, in 2000, it was reported that the company acquired in the neighborhood of 365 companies—the equivalent of an acquisition a day.

The empire came crashing down when Kozlowski was found to have avoided local sales tax by shipping empty boxes to his New Hampshire address, while the actual art was delivered to his Manhattan address. In a rapid succession of investigations, Kozlowski and his close deputies were found to have used hundreds of millions of dollars of company funds for personal purposes. Kozlowski and his former CFO are serving prison terms.

Bewildered Consumers

Ford/Firestone

In one of the most unusual crises—this involving two corporations battling each other in public—Ford Motor Company and Firestone Tires provided an ideal story for the media's appetite for the sensational.

When Ford discovered that a certain model of Firestone tire widely used on the popular Explorer model was defective, the missteps began. At first, Firestone announced it would immediately recall the tires in South America, because the problem was first discovered in Venezuela. They would get around to the rest of the hemisphere later. This did not sit well with U.S. consumers, who feared the worst. When Firestone announced free replacements of tires for everyone, consumers were shocked to find that, when they appeared at the dealers, the dealers knew nothing about the offer.

In the end, not only did Ford stop using the tires, but General Motors and Nissan curtailed their use as well.

Amid the public accusations of mismanagement flying between Ford and Firestone, it was clear that the public was quickly losing confidence because there was no assurance of an adequate supply of replacement tires. Promises of investigations were not sufficient. The public wanted new tires and wanted them immediately.

In the end, the company with the most at stake in the crisis, Firestone, was the most graphic failure, for it did not put customer safety first and was clearly unprepared to handle the most rudimentary aspects of the crisis—communications and logistics.

Pet Food Recall

In early 2007, devoted pet owners across the United States became concerned about the news of contaminated dog and cat food. As several pet deaths were reported, the list of affected brands grew almost daily. The brand manufacturers were as much the victims as the pets and their owners. Blame went to the supplier of raw materials, Canada's Menu Foods. In turn, accusations flew across the globe to China, where some of the raw materials originated. Brand by brand, products were recalled while the blame continued to circulate. The issue here is how to pinpoint blame in a complex supply chain—a tough question to answer while the public worries.

Attacks and Fraud in Cyberspace

The twenty-first century began with a crime unheard of just a decade earlier. Jonathan Leber, a fifteen-year-old New Jersey teenager, made nearly $275,000 in profits as the result of posting bogus information in chat rooms, driving up the price of various stocks in his portfolio. Leber became the first minor to ever be charged by the SEC with securities fraud. Though the crime was nothing new, the stunning reality was that it has been made simple by the existence of the PC and the web.

High Risk and Uncertainty

Union Carbide

In December 1984, two thousand people died when a Bhopal, India, chemical plant, owned 51 percent by Union Carbide, released a poison gas, methyl isocyanate (MIC). Another one hundred thousand to two hundred thousand people were blinded or otherwise injured.

The accident was the result of improper procedures, improper training, and slow reactions to warnings. Here was another example of a small problem escalating into disaster. When the initial leak was found, maintenance workers decided to wait until after their tea break to fix it. And when the alarms were sounded to warn of the break in the system, many workers ignored them—some thinking it was a drill.

When a similar incident at their Institute, West Virginia, plant occurred, Union Carbide first denied any similarities between the two releases, even hinting at sabotage. Trying to ease community concern, the company conducted a community town meeting, only to be fiercely criticized by angry and frightened neighbors. Only later did the company admit to multiple shortcomings in the operations.

After: The two events and the company's response had far-reaching implications for Union Carbide, whose chairman admitted that the company did not have a crisis plan. The CEO lost his job, and the company was ultimately acquired by a competitor.

The crisis has had far-reaching affects beyond Union Carbide as well. The Union Carbide tragedies and the media attention they received placed communities around the world, especially those with chemical plants in the backyards, on edge, while the chemical industry began taking a fresh look at community safety.

Three Mile Island Accident

The handling of the "meltdown" at Pennsylvania's Three Mile Island nuclear power plant in 1979, just a few years prior to the Tylenol scare, had a major negative impact on the nuclear industry, and serves as a textbook case for how not to handle a crisis. The facility was unprepared to communicate with the public and calm its fears, and so nationwide fear of a nuclear disaster arose. In the aftermath of the scare, nuclear power advocates began an extensive media campaign to convince the public that we need nuclear power and that it is safe. The campaign is a classic example of the wrong way to communicate risk to the public, including a public service announcement in which an actor portraying a scientist stood on the steps of the Lincoln Memorial and proclaimed (with no other explanation) that there is more radiation coming from the limestone in the memorial than from Three Mile Island. And what was the public's reaction? A continued distrust of the nuclear energy industry, and a potential newfound fear of visiting the Lincoln Memorial. A savvy public ignored the message.

Trapped on the Tarmac

Stories of airplanes stuck for hours on the tarmac in bad weather, filled to capacity with irate passengers, are not new, as Northwest Airlines and others made headlines several years ago. In the Northwest case, a determined passenger, using his cell phone, finally was able to reach the airline CEO at home, and then action was taken. An American Airlines pilot, tired of standing on the tarmac, finally moved his plane to an empty gate despite lack of authorization to do so.

In February 2007, icy weather and a good dose of play-by-the-book bureaucracy then brought JetBlue to its knees.

Some waits on the tarmac—only to fly nowhere—were up to eight hours, as toilets overflowed and passengers grew more and more agitated and hungry, wondering why buses could not be brought to the planes and everyone brought safely to the terminals.

The U.S. Department of Transportation now sets fines of as much as $27,500 per passenger when an airline leaves passengers stuck on a delayed plane for more than three hours. The rule applies to planes with more than thirty seats. *USA Today* reported in August 2012 that between January and June only four domestic U.S. flights sat on the tarmac for more than three hours. That compares with thirty-five delays for the same period the prior year.

4: Denial in the Land of Risk

Before 9/11, many Americans—and American businesses—thought of disasters as fires, explosions, and natural phenomena. Then 9/11 reached our collective psyches. Despite considerable efforts to encourage individuals and businesses to prepare for the new age of calamities, many are still in denial.

Whether the origins are terrorism or otherwise, the biggest concern now is cybersecurity.

Several myths or excuses stand in the way of business preparedness.

• Excuse No. 1:

It's expensive to create a plan.

Fact: Yes, it costs, but that expense is negligible compared to the cost of recovering from a crisis that could have been prevented or managed so that the losses and disruptions were minimal. The cost associated with a mismanaged crisis is far more than the actual expense of destroyed goods or idled labor. A company's most precious asset—its reputation, built carefully over the years—is on the line. It takes only one poorly managed crisis to send a company into a reputation tailspin from which it may never recover.

Nonetheless, economic shortsightedness continues to prevail in some quarters. "Left to their own devices, companies simply will not make the needed [security] investments," says Peter Navarro, economist at the University of California, Irvine. "That's the grim reality." ("Post-9/11: How Corporate America Responds," *Travel Vault*, National Business Travelers Association, undated)

• Excuse No. 2:

It won't happen here. Who cares about my company? We make boring products in an out of the way place.

Fact: The first reaction in many crises is denial—this cannot be happening. On any given day, bad things happen to good companies.

Everything from tornadoes to employee violence to acts of terrorism invades companies every day around the globe. And here's a surprising statistic: 91 percent of us live in areas that are considered high risk.

"Historically, humans get serious about avoiding disasters only after one has just smacked them in the face," notes *Time* magazine. "[A] review of the past year in disaster history suggests that modern Americans are particularly, mysteriously bad at protecting themselves from guaranteed threats. We know more than we ever did about the dangers we face. But it turns out that in times of crisis, our greatest enemy is rarely the storm, the quake or the surge itself. More often, it is ourselves."

(Amanda Ripley, "Floods, Tornadoes, Hurricanes, Wildfire, Earthquakes ... Why We Don't Prepare," *Time*, August 28, 2006)

Denial is not new in our society. Look at some of the nagging, chronic issues we face, such as problems of the homeless or gun violence. We tend to work at the edges of the problems but find no resolution. When we are in a fight for survival, however, we know how to act and to act fast. When we realized we needed to end World War II, the Manhattan Project was launched and the atomic bomb was developed at breakneck speed. Though the events of 9/11 in particular have led to protective changes, they are not enough.

- Excuse No. 3:

There is little proof or information about terrorist threats, so why should I get all worked up about the next terrorist attack?

Fact: There is ample evidence of terrorist activity around the world, even though official government sources can say very little. The war against terrorism is like no other, given the lack of contact with any leadership and the dispersed army of terrorists.

- Excuse No. 4:

There is no correlation between crisis preparation and stock price—which, after all, is all that matters.

Fact: Wall Street does not like uncertainty—especially a crisis not addressed head-on.

Wall Street punishes companies in crisis—and it happens quickly. Recovery to the pre-crisis level is a big challenge for some companies. While many recover, many others do not.

- Excuse No. 5:

Planning is complicated and time-consuming, and we just cannot afford the distraction.

Fact: You cannot afford not to. Once companies accept crisis planning as a normal part of their business, it becomes just that—a normal part of business. The more routine a company makes crisis planning, the more accepted and efficient it becomes, and the more protected your company is from the unexpected.

• Excuse No. 6:

I understand that once the plan is in place, we need to train our people. And if that's not enough, I hear we need to do periodic simulations. There is no way we can take the time!

Fact: Training, like all other aspects of crisis planning, can and should become a part of the company's routine. Simulations, whether annual or semiannual, are unusual and do disrupt the company routines for the time they take. The most effective ones do not exceed four hours plus another hour or two for debriefing to discuss lessons learned and steps for improvement. (The big war games you hear about are important, but leave those to the government agencies.)

There's an interesting plus to the simulations that I have noticed over the years. A company invariably discovers during a simulation a previously overlooked area of operations that, if corrected, may prevent a crisis.

The bottom line is simple. Every day spent in denial is a day a company places itself deeper into risky waters.

If your company needs further motivation, consider the competitive advantage of joining those companies that work every day to improve their crisis preparedness and leaving your competitors in the ranks of the unprepared. If nothing else motivates you to work on a crisis plan for your company on a calm day, then you may want to get to work on the explanations you will need to deliver to boards, shareholders, customers, government investigators, and the media in the midst of a crisis explaining why you were not prepared.

• Excuse No. 7:

Crises will happen, and there's nothing much you can do except wait for them to happen and then roll with the punches.

Fact: Many situations can be spotted before they become crises—if the right prevention and issue-management systems are in place.

• Excuse No. 8:

It's all about managing our reputation when a crisis hits. And we'll leave that to our PR department to take care of.

Fact: The PR department is a key component of every crisis plan and team. But the best PR people are not simply spin doctors. They are communications strategists and implementers. And they are able to tell, for example, about the actions being taken to resolve the crisis. The entire team needs to work on those actions.

• Excuse No. 9:

It's almost impossible to know where to start when looking for generally accepted rules for planning.

Fact: Since 9/11 the web has been filled with a Tower of Babble of guidance and information from the U.S. government, the American Red Cross, and virtually every professional and trade association. Most of it is quite good, but the abundance of all of this information—without some ranking or analysis by a business equivalent of Consumer Reports—leaves planners adrift. All the while, the much-touted NFPA 1600 has emerged as a step toward an official guidepost. This document, drawn up by the National Fire Protection Association, is an exhaustive checklist for mid-level crisis managers.

• Excuse No. 10:

No one made me prepare.

Fact: Does your board care about the company's reputation? If it does, it should include crisis prevention and readiness as a governance issue.

Norman Augustine, former CEO of Lockheed Martin, put it very well in "How to Turn a Crisis into a Catastrophe in 12 Easy Steps."

Assume the evidence of the problem must be wrong.

When evidence mounts, cover up the problem.

Let the lawyers manage the response strategy—admit nothing.

When the problem becomes public, minimize it.

Never display remorse; blame someone else, preferably the victim.

Take plenty of time to study the problem.

Have the highest-level responsible individual go into hiding.

Attack the media.

Anger the regulators, preferably by embracing untenable positions.

Shift the spotlight to the failing of the regulators.

Frequently reverse your position and contradict yourself.

Give priority to saving money on the front end—that way you have more to lose later.

(Norman Augustine, "Report of the National Association of Corporate Directors Blue Ribbon Commission on Risk Oversight," 2002)

• Excuse No. 11:

In a disaster, the government will take over and manage everything. So why should our company bother with a crisis plan?

Fact: The government cannot and will not do everything. While it appears that reforms have been put in place since the government malfunction in the aftermath of Hurricane Katrina, do not expect the government to be all-compassing in its management of a disaster. As George Foresman, former undersecretary for the Department of Homeland Security's Preparedness Directorate, put it:

"Government will be able to do as much as it can reasonably do in the aftermath of an emergency or disaster. But we have not built our government structures nor does business have a motivational incentive to construct our systems and our processes to be able to deal with a full range of emergencies and disasters that potentially will confront this nation. In other words, we're not going to always have shelter for 1.8 million people at the ready, ready to flip a switch to turn it on.

"We are not going to have in place transportation resources that could quickly, in twenty-four hours or less, move hundreds of thousands of people from a major metropolitan area to other areas in the aftermath of an emergency or disaster." (Address by George Foresman to the U.S. Chamber of Commerce, Washington, D.C., June 1, 2006)

The simple, most difficult reality is that we do not know when or where the next act of terrorism or any other crisis may occur, but we can be prepared to deal with it effectively, if we remember all the details—including the "I forgots."

An examination of how to avoid some of the most common omissions can help keep any company on the road to continuous improvement and readiness:

(1) Find the crisis plan. Is the plan easily accessible? Does everyone have a copy? When you need the basics, including the checklists for what everyone needs to remember to do, there is no time for hunting through the shelves and computer files. Where are the phone numbers for key personnel? Where are the e-mail addresses? The best advice: Keep the crisis plan short, preferably on a folded card that fits in a pocket or briefcase. Keep it updated with all the vital contact information. And keep at least one copy of the names and numbers in your wallet or briefcase and on your iPad and smartphone.

(2) Conduct an annual checkup. Ordinary change is a constant threat to your crisis plan. Personnel turnover can be a major problem. You've got to monitor staff changes and train new members of the crisis teams. A more complex problem comes when businesses and their infrastructures grow or consolidate. This is where crisis plans can easily be forgotten. No company should ever permit a merger or acquisition to relegate the crisis plan to the "forgotten" bin. The best advice: Schedule your annual crisis plan review soon, and stick with it.

(3) Designate backups. Who is traveling, on vacation, or out sick? Inevitably, someone on the crisis team is not available when the worst hits. The best advice: Designate backups for every position—and make sure they all are up to speed on how to perform the job.

(4) Remember that employees are important. Do you have a system in place to quickly determine the whereabouts and safety of every employee—at the plant, at the office, at off-site meetings, and while traveling? Do you have emergency food and other supplies on hand in the event of a shelter-in-place situation? Do you have flashlights and other evacuation aids on hand in some ready-to-use kits? And do you have a communication system in place to ensure that employees are notified of crisis news as quickly and directly as possible so they do not hear it first on Twitter or TV or radio broadcasts—or via frantic phone calls from loved ones? The best advice: Don't wait. Put the right tracking alert systems in place as soon as possible.

(5) Commit to practice, practice, and more practice. All too often practice sessions are postponed for budget or scheduling reasons. Or they are forgotten altogether. These sessions are invaluable, often critical, reminders of what needs to be done through real-world practice. Inevitably, simulations also have tangible results because they identify areas that need fixing or improvement to either prevent or better manage a crisis.

5: It's About CEO Leadership and Communication

"I do solemnly pledge to uphold and protect the reputation of this corporation and all its brands. In fact, the buck stops here."

Make no mistake—you are in the biggest fishbowl. When disaster strikes, the eyes of the media will be on you. And you avoid these eyes at your peril.

At the end of the day, it is the reputation of the brand or the company or both that are at stake in a crisis. What is this intangible asset called reputation? It is the total of what various people think about your company or brands or both. Would they buy shares in the company? Would they buy the products over the competitors'? Would they come to work at your company if you offered them a job?

Most CEOs, when asked who is responsible for the reputation of their company, say it is theirs. If reputation is to be preserved in a crisis, a rock-solid, tested crisis prevention and response plan is essential to that responsibility.

But who "gets it" and who does not?

Which one are you?

There are the visionaries—the CEOs in the small, medium, and large companies who know that crisis preparation pays. They are in the minority.

Others are in denial. Let's call them the avoiders—the ones who say, "It won't happen here. And by the way, the expense of crisis readiness is an easy expense to cut. After all, no one's really going to hold me accountable"—unless it hits the fan.

Then there are the vulnerables—the leaders of companies in high-risk industries or high-risk locations that are so well prepared they beat all odds and become the heroes when a worst-case disaster strikes. The most recent examples are those that survived when Hurricane Katrina and then Hurricane Rita struck the Gulf region in two of the worst natural disasters our country has ever faced.

According to Ambassador L. Paul Bremer III, "Large corporations can expect to face a crisis on average every four or five years. . . . [E]very CEO will probably have to manage at least one crisis during their tenure. A director may face two or three crises during a normal tour of service on a board." (L. Paul Bremer III, "Corporate Governance and Crisis Management," Director and Boards, Winter 2002)

Mistakes and crises will occur. You and the company will be judged not on the mistakes, but on what you have done about them—specifically, what steps have been taken to prevent the same problem.

The Power of the CEO

Executive power has the capacity for effective crisis planning.

You can put together the best plan, train the staff, and wait. Then, when you think you've got the best plan, it happens anyway. And it can happen—because even the best of plans cannot govern the far-flung reaches of today's global corporation. Faced with the challenge of managing from afar, here are a few hints that can help to minimize these problems:

- Visit
- Communicate
- Share plans and updates constantly
- Listen
- Reward

According to Wayne A. Hochwarter, associate professor of management at Florida State University's College of Business, "[C]risis planning . . . and sharing the plans with employees . . . has a substantial effect on worker attitudes." These include:

- Significantly higher levels of job satisfaction
- Greater willingness to do things beyond what is expected by management
- Perception of greater control
- More enthusiasm and a greater willingness to work harder than expected
- More compassion for others
- Greater feelings of support from the organization

- Increase in employees' sense of importance and a building of camaraderie
- Lower levels of depressed mood at work

("Research Identifies an Intrinsic Benefit of Continuity Planning," Continuity Central, September 6, 2006)

"From Churchill to Giuliani, the leaders who are most effective in crisis are most visible. Whether in person or via other means of communication, leaders must appear engaged, available, and in touch. The temptation, or even the necessity, to stay in the office revising budgets and hashing out strategy must be balanced with the need to connect directly with staff, constituents, customers, and others who expect to see their leaders in action.

Effective leaders in challenging situations also demonstrate optimism that the challenge will be met successfully, but do not downplay the difficulties. Leaders should keep in mind that fear and pessimism are contagious, particularly when they come from those in charge. At the same time, leaders who sugarcoat bad news or dismiss the obstacles lose credibility." (Wick Keating, "Does History Provide any Guidance?," *Catalyst*, Winter 2002)

If and when a crisis strikes, when does the CEO speak? Or does the CEO speak? There is growing recognition that the public persona and public conduct of the CEO is a primary factor for success. The *Wall Street Journal* compared GE's successor to the legendary Jack Welch, Jeff Immelt, with the guy who lost, Bob Nardelli. Nardelli went on to become CEO of The Home Depot, then was fired in 2007.

"Messrs. Nardelli and Immelt are the Cain and Abel of the corporate world—both groomed for greatness by Mr. Welch but divided when their mentor had to choose. Mr. Immelt is tall and smooth, a graduate of Dartmouth and Harvard. Mr. Nardelli is short and gruff, with degrees from Western Illinois and Louisville universities . . . [F]or better or worse it is a much more public game, involving a wide range of constituencies and requiring the skills of a politician." (Alan Murray, "A Tale of Two CEOs: How Public Perception Shapes Reputations," *Wall Street Journal*, July 13, 2006)

Is it that simple? What do we really mean when we talk about communication skills and persona as critical attributes? Yes, they are critical—but they do not stand alone. They are part of a complex of factors that, over the years, have evolved despite changing fashions in management.

What, then, are the attributes of an effective CEO, once we strip away the fads and the pontifications of management gurus?

He or she:

• Knows that failures provide great management lessons. (Just don't repeat the same mistake twice.) A crisis may be the greatest test for the CEO and even the life of the brand or the company.

• Knows that leadership involves equal parts of decisiveness and listening. According to the late Peter Drucker, "The issues facing management don't change from year to year. The answers do. The biggest skill needed to address these issues is not really a skill—it is a basic attitude, a willingness to start not with the question, 'What do I want to do?,' but with the question 'What needs to be done?' It was the willingness to ask this question that made the fairly mediocre Harry Truman a great president and the superbly gifted Richard Nixon a failure." (Michael V. Copeland, "How to Succeed in 2005," *Business 2.0*, December 2004)

• Appreciates, respects and mentors subordinates.

• Understands the role of the board—as stewards and strategists.

• Is scrupulously honest and has earned the trust of employees and customers. As J & J's Jim Burke said: "If you run a public company, you cannot ignore the public. Institutional trust is far more important than most people realize. The operative word is trust . . . and whether people will take one's word when one badly needs them to do so will depend on how much confidence has been built in the organization over the years before the crisis occurs." (Norman R. Augustine, "Managing the Crisis You Tried to Prevent")

• Understands that the public expects and respects transparency. In a world exploding with social media and the electronics to spread the words of deeds and misdeeds in a blink, transparency—holding the company up to the light—can be an advantage or a liability.

• Is a superb communicator—to employees, customers, investors, and the media. Wondering how much to say? Warren Buffet's advice is clear: "First, state clearly that you do not know all the facts. Then promptly state the facts you do know. One's objective should be to get it right, get it quick, get it out, and get it over. You see, your problem won't improve with age."

(Norman R. Augustine, "Managing the Crisis You Tried to Prevent," *Harvard Business Review*, November-December 1995)

A crisis is a time when the CEO must make it clear that he or she is in charge. While it may seem obvious, it is important to assert this leadership quickly and clearly.

GE's Jeff Immelt, who has won praise for his management style, offers some criteria that apply to crisis management:

"Simplify constantly. Stay true to your own style. 'Every morning,' says Immelt, 'I look in the mirror and say, "I could have done three things better yesterday . . .

"And 'Leave a few things unsaid. I may know an answer, but I'll often let the team find its own way. Sometimes, being an active listener is much more effective than ending a meeting with me enumerating seventeen actions.' " (John A. Byme, "Practicing More than Jack Preached," *Fast Company*, April 2004)

• Has high energy, and knows how to balance that energy between the job and personal life. "The first essential trait of leadership," according to Jack and Suzy Welch, "is positive energy—the capacity to go-go-go with healthy vigor and an upbeat attitude toward good times and bad. The second is the ability to energize others, releasing their positive energy, to take any hill. The third trait is edge—the ability to make tough calls, to say yes or no, not maybe. The fourth trait is the talent to execute—very simply, to get things done. Fifth and finally, leaders have passion. They care deeply. They sweat; they believe." (Jack Welch and Suzy Welch, *Winning*, HarperCollins, 2005)

• Knows how to balance time in a crisis—especially the early hours or days when confusion is more common than order. The CEO, who is the presumed crisis team leader, needs to manage time so that morale is maintained, the media are fed, and a strategy is developed.

Peter Drucker gave some advice on managing CEO time:

"[I]t is my observation that effective executives do have in common certain practices or habits—and practices can be learned. One obvious practice is the conservation of time. In a peculiar way the executive's time is everybody else's time but his own. Everybody can move in on him, and usually everybody does. He cannot shut himself off from these demands, but he must use the little time he can control to do the important things. This is the secret of those few people who accomplish so much with so little apparent effort. They put first things first." (Peter Drucker, "Advice From the Master," *Fortune*, December 12, 2005)

• Has the right people on the crisis team. And the best team includes those who are confident to voice their opinions, get things done, and stay focused. In the early hours of a crisis, when strategies are being developed, the best team leader listens to all ideas.

• Remembers that the best spokespersons prepare to face the media. Always have some coaching/rehearsal time before the media invasion.

• Has a strong understanding of and commitment to crisis prevention, preparation, and response. And when it does hit the fan, is ready and able to remain calm and direct the company toward fast response.

• Is willing to take responsible risks, recognizing the risk/benefit ratios—which are subjective—and the consequences for brand and company reputation, the balance sheet and share price.

• Believes that the following three points will guide the way:

(1) Crisis readiness is not a sometimes thing, relegated to a security or facilities officer. It is a primary corporate function, managed by a senior company officer who reports directly to the CEO.

(2) The only valid crisis plan is a short one that fits into your pocket and your smartphone and iPad.

(3) A commitment to several simulations a year is an immovable commitment that yields the benefits of increased readiness and the bonus of discovering actions to continuously improve readiness or in fact to prevent some crises.

• Resists bureaucracy.

• Is ready—really ready—to hear bad news.

• Has the loyalty of key employees—Listens to a balanced spectrum of problem-solving strategies and the latest one-size-fits-all management fad, and then considers the pros and cons of all.

• Is up to date on what the competition is doing.

• Understands and is able to balance the often conflicting advice of the lawyers and the communicators.

There has been debate for years over who has the upper hand in communicating during a crisis—the corporate communications department or the legal department. The CEO and the crisis team need to face this dilemma. Most lawyers will advocate saying as little as possible, and the communicators will want to communicate as much as possible. If the facts are concrete, there is a great deal to be gained by communicating openly and quickly—in fact, it may save lives and brand reputation.

These lawyer vs. communicator conflicts can be minimized by coming to terms on ground rules in advance of a crisis, and incorporating those ground rules into the crisis plan.

While we are on the subject of the lawyers, we need to recognize that lawyers often are the first to know of an issue or brewing problem that may escalate into a crisis. It is in the best interests of everyone to include the communicators as early as possible. Here are ten indicators that lawyers ought to bring in the communicators:

(1) The media are knocking at the door.
(2) Rumors are afloat.
(3) Some employees know about the problem, and others surely will know soon.
(4) It will take time and intense effort to put a communications strategy, key messages, and action plan in place.
(5) The CEO and other key personnel need to be coached and trained to act as the spokespersons.
(6) Third-party spokespersons will be crucial allies when or if the issue becomes public—and they will need to be identified.
(7) The company is publicly traded, and news of the problem has the potential to affect share price.
(8) News may leak at any time.
(9) You've never met the communications staff or outside consultants, and they do not have a clue on the issue.
(10) The company or brand reputation is potentially at stake.

• Knows there are times when it is advisable to admit mistakes and apologize.

It may take fifteen seconds to deliver an apology. But an arrogant statement or lack of apology or contrition may require fifteen years for recovery.

When a CEO or other senior executive communicates in a crisis, there is often the question of whether or not to apologize and when. An apology, according to the American Heritage Dictionary, is ". . . an acknowledgment expressing regret or asking pardon for a fault or offense."

While some lawyers are cautious about the implications of apologizing for a crisis, there is a growing school of thought that an apology or some form of expression of regret over a crisis has a proper place in how a leader communicates in a crisis.

When carefully worded to avoid liability or premature admissions of guilt before the facts behind a crisis are determined, there is a great deal to be said for expressions of sympathy, empathy, and concern.

Consider that an apology does the following things:

(1) Calms agitated customers. Look at a situation we all have faced: a flight delay. The gate agent changes the departure board to show a ninety-minute delay, then disappears. Anger mounts, rumors circulate. Now consider another agent who, on posting the new time, makes an announcement: "We apologize for the delay. Weather in Chicago has delayed the arrival of inbound aircraft, but it should be here in sixty minutes. The weather forecast in Chicago is looking quite good now, and we should be ready to leave in ninety minutes. Thanks for your patience." You now know the situation, the mystery has been solved. Your blood pressure is coming down.

(2) Shows respect for the public. The public is savvy, possessing a certain "street-smartness" or skepticism born of the TV and social media in which successes and failures are instantly brought to us. More often than not, the public reacts positively to honest, clear communication. But they also hold companies accountable if they're not treated with respect and honesty. The public, when faced with news of difficult times for a company or brand—especially if employees or customers are affected—wants to hear that the company is concerned with the problem, has a commitment to finding the facts and fixing the problem, and is willing to explain what actions are being taken and what others are planned.

(3) Puts a human face on an otherwise anonymous corporation. This is especially important given the increasing anonymity of technology and the "Press '1' if you know your party's extension" world. You may not know every detail of the crisis, but you are the senior face of the organization—and as we learned from the Exxon Valdez situation, there is a lot to be said about the presence of the CEO in times of crisis. Your presence sends a clear message to employees, the community, and the public, that you care and that you are accountable for the resolution of the crisis.

The delivery of an apology is one of the toughest moments in the life of a CEO, but there is evidence that beneficial effects of an apology can even be measured. Barbara Kellerman, in a *Harvard Business Review* article, observed: "In a recent British study of malpractice patients, 37 percent said they never would have gone to court in the first place had an explanation and an apology been extended." (Barbara Kellerman, "When Should a Leader Apologize and When Not?," *Harvard Business Review*, April 2006))

People will react differently to apologies. Some will accept, some will reject. In some cases, costly legal battles can be avoided. Retailer Eddie Bauer was caught in an embarrassing situation when one of its store security guards accused an African-American teenager of stealing a shirt when in reality the young man had purchased the shirt the day before. No apologies were offered. The family sued in what became a costly lawsuit for Eddie Bauer. The teenager's father stated, "If they had apologized from the start or given some response, the lawsuit wouldn't happen. It feels like they don't care."

Consider some ways of expressing concern and an apology: "I understand how frustrating this must be." "I want to assure you of our deepest regret for this inconvenience. Now I would like to explain the steps we are taking to protect our customers."

And above all, keep it simple!

"Consumers are ready to forgive companies, but only if they think that an apology is sincere and is accompanied by corrective action," said Gavin Fitzsimmons, associate professor of marketing at Duke University's Fuqua School of Business. The *Washington Post*, he points out, observed at the time that ". . . what Johnson & Johnson executives have done is communicate the message that the company is candid, contrite and compassionate, committed to solving the murders and protecting the public." (Robert J. Bliwise, "We Apologize: The Sorry State of Remorse," *Duke*, May-June 2004)

Ask yourself the following questions when deciding on whether to issue an apology:

• Will I be protecting my own integrity?

• Is there ample evidence or sentiment among stakeholders that people are angry and have suffered some degree of harm?

• Will the apology accomplish anything? Will it, for example, calm some nerves, or serve as an introduction of a statement of what is happening?

• If I do not apologize, will anger and rumors increase?

Does a CEO need to have charisma?

Andy Gilman, who trained J&J chairman Jim Burke during the Tylenol tampering, and who has trained thousands of executives since, says that, "Very few people have charisma. Bill Clinton is clearly one—no matter your politics—who has it."

If you don't have the natural charisma, you can still create a better presence. It's lots of little things like handshakes, eye contact, clothing, smiling when you meet others, saying something positive about people you meet, and expressing concern and curiosity.

When should the CEO speak?

Gilman also observed, "This was one of the most unique crises in that J&J did nothing wrong. In most other crises, there is—as the lawyers say—contributory negligence. While most companies don't deliberately do anything wrong, when a ship runs aground, that's the company's fault. When the food is tainted, it's a company-caused accident. When the engineer falls asleep on the train, that's a company problem. In this case, J&J didn't do anything wrong.

"J&J's famous Credo meant something," Gilman adds. "There was a value system in place. They also had goodwill deposits in their PR bank. They did make smart decisions. They pulled a strong team together and worked on it. They went above and beyond what they had to do. The government did not require tamper-proof packaging and at first not triplicate seals. And once they had answers and solutions they were very aggressive and proactive in their communications efforts."

" 'Putting a leader's face on crisis response is almost a necessity now, whether for potentially fatal product flaws or annoyances like flight delays,' said Sue Parenio, an associate professor of advertising at Boston University. 'Americans are so fed up with poor treatment from large corporate bureaucracies,' she said, 'that they will accept reassurance only from the top official.' " (Julie Flaherty, "The Contrite CEO," *New York Times*, September 3, 2000)

Some leaders rise to the occasion on the spot. While the concentration here is on the business side, not the government, it is all but impossible to ignore the calming leadership of Mayor Rudy Giuliani on 9/11 and in the days and months following the collapse of the World Trade Center. His ability to calm all of New York City and the surrounding area, to console the bereaved, and to encourage everyone to return to their normal lives—preventing the terrorists from saying they had won—will be part of history.

Some of the questions to ask to help make the decision on CEO availability as leading spokesperson:

- Where are the media? Does it look like there is national or international media interest?
- What is the extent of the crisis? Are there extensive injuries or fatalities?
- Has extensive harm been done either to a company site or the surrounding community?
- How long will it take to get to the crisis site?
- If I leave, am I confident in my deputy to carry on in the crisis room?
- Will I jump in too quickly before we know if this is a full-blown crisis? If I jump in too quickly, I could help elevate what is now an emergency into a full-blown crisis.

But the time has come to add an important concept to the requirements of what makes an effective CEO: How does he act under the pressure of a crisis?

Under pressure, the CEO is the compass to whom everyone turns. He or she must know what to say that will provide the facts, convey compassion, and a determination that resilience and resources will resolve the crisis.

6: The Media—Big Pluses, Big Minuses

The media keep us connected and informed; they report the sensational, and they can be superficial as well. While the traditional media are going through great changes in the midst of social media growth and changing reader habits, the *New York Times*, the *Wall Street Journal*, the *Financial Times*, and the best of TV news still carry weight.

The media play a central role in any company's crisis response. They are demanding; and they are self-appointed investigators. They can be your effective messengers, or they can be your nagging enemy. Or both.

The media today are increasingly diverse and aggressive in their quest for bad news—and those companies that are able to protect their reputations and share price during a crisis are the ones that understand the media, understand the need to be open and responsive to the media, and are able to gain some control over the process.

The media today have greater speed and greater reach than ever, adding a new meaning to the phrase "mass media." Mass now means potentially reaching every person on Earth, either directly or indirectly, with the speed of light.

The best of today's journalists, editors and columnists understand the roots of good journalism. A good example is the late Walter Cronkite, who at his peak was known as the most trusted person in America.

I was fortunate, early in my career at CBS, to be part of the Cronkite team for political and space coverage. The work included the "get this done" assignments reserved for a junior staffer; and it involved quite a bit of travel and the ability to work with Cronkite up close.

The space launches from Cape Canaveral were perhaps highest on his list of passions, and he was in his element there.

A star? In every respect, but by no means a prima donna. Demanding? Yes. Especially when it came to the facts. He was not about to let his viewers down.

Anchoring space coverage in the pre-laptop and smartphone days, he traveled to Cape Canaveral with very extensive files on every aspect of space coverage. On one launch the plan was for him to leave the TV anchor booth at Cape Canaveral immediately following liftoff and fly by small private jet to Houston to continue coverage. He declared he would need his four-drawer steel file cabinet, filled to the brim, on the plane with him, ready for the resumption of his reporting in Houston. I gasped when I thought of the weight, but the pilot agreed it would be worth a try. I will always remember the suspense as I stood on the runway watching takeoff— as the plane did not lift off till the last few feet of runway remained. But Walter Cronkite made it to Houston, and with his files intact.

He wanted these files. They included every conceivable fact and factoid—from astronaut bios to critical dates and every imaginable fact about outer space. The files gave him the assurance he could communicate on virtually any aspect of the space shot. And he used them, providing the succinct, absorbing delivery of the news we all knew then and now were the hallmark of what journalism is all about.

Times have changed since CBS News was the place to be and the place for news. But Walter's influence is there for those who either witnessed him or studied him. For those who have not, it is their loss. Though the way we receive news now is split among 24/7 cable news, the networks, PBS, the web, and social media, the influences are there.

Throughout all the media choices, the best communication will be based, as Cronkite knew so well, on the depth of facts. Without the facts, reporting—or in fact any communication regarding an issue—is shallow and of no value. In a crisis-prone world we need no less.

The media play a significant role in perpetuating (and sometimes creating) crises. The growth in mass communication has created intense competition among media outlets for swift headlines, which leads to occasional lapses in standards. While the media overwhelmingly provide responsible, urgent information to the public, they also continue to be cited for being too quick on occasion to rely on "sources," and often report on the latest scientific and opinion surveys without thoroughly vetting the sources or the information.

Today's media, more than ever, are incredibly diverse—from the in-depth, serious news coverage of the PBS *NewsHour* to the sensational, this-just-in scandal of the day reported by CNN's Nancy Grace. The rise of social media and the 24/7 news throughout the TV channels, on the web, and on smartphone and iPad apps have changed the face of news reporting, providing us with news when it happens and when we want it, and in small, easy-to-digest doses.

With the enormous panorama of competition for our eyes and ears, some of the media are on the decline as they struggle to keep our attention and sell advertising.

The morning TV shows—*Today*, *CBS Morning*, *Good Morning America* and *Morning Joe* often hit the right buttons with an attractive mix of breaking news and discussions. CNN and FoxNews bet on the sensational with a few prime-time exposé shows. Newspapers struggle and consolidate. The venerable *New York Times* maintains its mission of presenting "all the news that's fit to print" while trying some edgier coverage and features, and the *Wall Street Journal* has lightened up with an array of personal features.

Local TV news remains as aggressive as ever. The ten o'clock news on the stations in Washington, D.C., and New York owned by Metromedia (now Fox), pioneered the "if it bleeds, it leads" strategy, and hundreds of other local TV news shows have followed suit with reports of daily rapes, murders, or fires.

Howard Kurtz, the *Washington Post*'s media correspondent, described the changed landscape well:

"I like being able to click on newspapers from around the world, see bloggers smack each other around, google any person or thing that pops into my brain, watch news videos (and some stupid stuff too) on YouTube, and generally surf till I drop." (Howard Kurtz, "Ink-Stained to Link-Stained: A Kvetch," *Washington Post*, December 25, 2006)

Technology—from smartphones to iPads—has changed our lives too. I can conduct business on an iPad —on the beach at 6 A.M., in the North Sea in the middle of the night, and sitting at my desk. I routinely answer e-mails from London on the way to the Metro in the morning. And no one on the other end has any idea where I am.

Kurtz continues, "Now, liberated from the stronghold of CBS, NBC, and ABC, we can watch news channels that match our political predilections, read websites that reinforce our opinions, stream our favorite radio talkers through our computer speakers, download videos that mirror our obsessions, and select songs for our iPod playlists. . . . [W]e can get anything we want, at the precise moment we want it, tailored to our merest whim." (Howard Kurtz, "Ink-Stained to Link-Stained: A Kvetch")

I thought I had a good chunk of my daily research under control when I signed on with CNN for news alerts. I was getting news of the terrorist arrests, presidential press conferences, and even hurricane warnings. Then this popped up, as "breaking news," on my phone: odd items of celebrity sightings and marriage travails as news alerts. Just another sign of the change in the definition of news.

Amid all the headlines today, business news has become a steady part of the news diet. Where business news was once considered dull and the job of the once-stuffy business papers, it is now mainstream news, helped along by the steady stream of scandals and by the realization that more Americans—including the average Joe and Jane—are shareholders in America's corporations, and they want to know what is going on.

Some of it even goes to extremes—as in the phenomenon of cable's Jim Kramer, a shouting, screaming reporter who chronicles the stock market news as if he were reporting the Super Bowl or a wrestling match. He's smart. You just need to tolerate the hysteria pitch.

Along comes your crisis, and the media are all over you—especially if the news is visual and has some real or suspected element of scandal. And everyone wants to be first with the news or the interview, including the newspapers, which no longer are dependent only on the delivery of the morning paper at the front door. They are updating their websites as the news pours in.

As Tim Wagner, American Airlines' webmaster, reflecting on the events of 9/11, put it, "AMR's [parent company of American Airlines] crisis communications plan calls for 'communicating aggressively online' because it is much more efficient than other media. If we can answer on the website the questions everyone asks, it frees our people to answer different questions over the telephone." (Tom Price, "Public Affairs Strategies in the Internet Age," The Foundation for Public Affairs, 2002)

With all these choices, consider some facts about how Americans—the Americans we want to understand our issues—are getting their news today.

For the TV viewers, Fox News is gaining steadily, with more than half of their viewers describing themselves as politically conservative, while

CNN's audience leans more to the liberal. NPR, not surprisingly, also shows more liberal fans.

When news of a disaster strikes, the media are attracted like magnets and want instant answers, quotes from the biggest players they can get. And if the disaster satisfies their hunger for a story affecting people is also highly visual for TV and is easy to understand, they will not go away until the crisis ends. In the hunt for headlines and continuing coverage, they will look for the sensational and will play amateur detective, looking to fix blame. This simply is a fact of life—and one that will not change. It places a very special burden on the company in crisis to speak out quickly, truthfully, and frequently. If you do not become part of the media mix in the first moments of your crisis, the media will find others to comment on your situation. You won't like it, and it will take great pains to catch up.

For all news sources, there is a steady increase in international interest—no surprise, as terrorism and wars continue.

And social media—the tweets, Facebook postings, and other sites—that a few years ago were mostly the news sources for younger people, are also attracting more interest from seniors and minorities. This is a natural evolution.

Newspaper readership is the big divide. Six in ten people over sixty-five say they read a newspaper each day. Under thirty? Only 23 percent report they read a paper. And across all demographics, newspapers are finding an increasing online readership. The *New York Times*, for example, attracts 1.5 million online readers each day, compared to one million for the paper edition.

And who among the public are the most knowledgeable when it comes to current affairs? Readers of *The New Yorker* and *The Atlantic*.

Well, you get the picture.

And this is an important picture, because we need to be aware, from an issue point of view, of how the grassroots—the voters, the supporters and opponents of your issues—are getting their news and information.

Except for newspapers, publications like *The New Yorker* and *The Atlantic*, and the *NewsHour* on PBS, most of the news is coming to us in shorter chunks—the two-minute story on the TV news, or 140 characters in a tweet. Want more? Click on it. But not every headline earns a click.

What does all this mean for us—especially if we are trying to persuade the public to understand our point of view in a crisis?

The answer is: Keep it simple, keep it short. This task is not as simple as it sounds—you need to avoid oversimplification while keeping it simple. As Mark Twain is reported to have said when admonished by an editor for the length of a manuscript: "If I'd had more time, it would have been shorter."

Blogs continue to attract huge interest. Is it justified? Well, maybe—and maybe not. According to Wikipedia.org, a blog (short for web log) is "a web page that serves as a publicly-accessible personal journal for an individual. Typically updated daily, blogs often reflect the personality of the author."

As a news source it is important to judge the content based on its source. Unlike a trusted media source such as the *New York Times*, blogs have no executive editors.

Some people blog for personal reasons, expressing themselves. Others have a deeper agenda to take on issues and causes. In the long run, blogging is here to stay. It is likely blogging will take many shapes and stay with us as another form of communication.

While companies are increasingly monitoring blogs and what they say about their companies and brands, the most prevalent use of blogs is in the political arena. We should not ignore them. This ultimate democratic communication tool will be useful.

The consumer blogs are among the most prolific. You can go online and check what people are saying about a restaurant, a hotel, a product, etc. TripAdvisor.com, for example, can make or break a hotel. On the consumer product side, online shopping has become easier. Confronted with choosing among two dozen digital recorders on Amazon.com, I easily chose the one I did because a previous customer had said, "Even my mother can figure this one out."

If you're tempted to start a company blog, remember:

• Have a good reason. Answering angry customers could be a reason—but remember that what you say and how you say it reflects on the entire company.

• Keep it simple and easy to navigate.

• This is all permanent stuff. Once you've done it, it does not go away.

Pete Snyder, former president of New Media Strategies and one of the pioneers in advising companies on the blog phenomenon, put it this way:

"The worst possible thing for a company to do in the face of constant criticism is to take the imperial ivory tower 'we don't respond' tack, otherwise known as the 'head in sand' ostrich strategy, which allows critics to control the conversation and amplify what should have been a teapot tempest into a full-blown riot. If the basis for attacks on a company is false, it is critical to address them in forums, via company blogs, and social media. Consumers don't read press releases, and it is critical to get the other side of a story to them in the same format that they are encountering negative news. When presented with the facts in a plainspoken, straightforward manner, online communities usually squash untrue rumors at an astonishing speed.

"If however, the accusations that are being leveled against a firm are at the end of the day valid, a different communication strategy is needed. First, acknowledging the problem is key—customers appreciate honesty and the recognition that they've been heard. Second is presenting a plan on how it will be addressed, or if it can't be resolved, an open and honest explanation of why not. Lastly, providing updates on a regular basis lets the public know that the issue hasn't fallen off the radar screen." (Interview with author)

The media trend these days is to do instant polling on CNN, NBC's *Today Show*, and others. "Go online and tell us what you think of this or that." Is this valid? I think not—those who cast the votes are self-selecting based on their inclination to cast a vote, whether they have the time do so, etc. Be wary of these polls. They may be fun, but they are not valid samples.

Apart from the gathering of information on an issue you already know exists, what is the value of monitoring the media? It has enormous value in issue detection and preventing an issue from becoming a crisis. Consider, for example, all the information you can gather from news coverage and reports of how another company or industry has faced an issue. And with this information, ask yourself the tough questions. Could this happen here? If it did could we handle it, and how? Are we vulnerable too? And if we are, what can we do about this early warning right now?

The Tylenol tamperings proved that the media can create an instant hero, as they did with Jim Burke, J&J's chairman. Burke was perfect. These were unsolved murders. The product was very popular, and Burke was Mr. Sincere and Mr. Caring—the uncle next door. The alternative is to create an instant symbol of the uncaring corporation, as in the case of Lawrence Rawl, Exxon's CEO, who, in the Valdez oil spill crisis, avoided the media at the expense of the corporation's reputation. Or BP's Tony Hayward, who is remembered most for saying, "I want my life back."

Part II

Closing The Readiness Gap

7: A Prescription for 100 Percent Protection and Readiness

"The only thing harder than planning for an emergency is explaining why you didn't."
—*Anonymous*

There is a "readiness gap" of at least 25 percent in our nation's private-sector crisis preparedness. The sad truth is that our collective level of denial is way too high for today's high-risk world. Until there is clear accountability and in some cases financial incentives—whether driven by boards who demand crisis planning as part of CEO salary and bonus, insurance premium incentives, or tax breaks—we will continue to have a checkerboard of companies in varying states of readiness. Only the visionaries and the vulnerables who have been through the worst of the worst disasters will have the will to be ready.

The real truth—what should be the best incentive for preparation—also lies in the all-important share price for publicly traded companies. There is frequently a correlation between high-profile crises and a decline in share price. And many companies—the unprepared—never recover.

After thirty-plus years of development, the specialty of crisis management is ripe to become a profession. This will come about through the creation of a professional organization—for the sake of discussion, let's call this yet-to-be-created organization the International Crisis Management Institute—and an accelerated effort to push crisis management to become a corporate governance issue. This will not be an easy task, but the time has come to begin. It first will require leadership—

from government, the law, companies, and the crisis management profession.

Despite thousands of how-to efforts—not least of which is the Department of Homeland Security's Ready.gov—there are no pressures and incentives to close the 25 percent gap. If crisis readiness among American business continues to improve at roughly 2 percent a year, we may easily be looking at another dozen-plus years before we are 100 percent crisis-ready. That rate of improvement is unacceptable.

It's going to take accountability and it's going to take a professional approach to standards and training.

Moving to the 100 percent level will require:

• Accelerated efforts to convince board members that crisis readiness is a corporate governance issue

• Shareholder efforts to hold corporations accountable for crisis planning

• The creation of an international standards and training institute

First Steps

A number of efforts are under way to create generally accepted standards, through the International Standards Organization and others. One of the most ambitious efforts to create national standards for crisis readiness and response has been the work by the National Fire Protection Association. The standards document, called NFPA 1600, is, according to NFPA, a "Standard on Disaster/Emergency Management and Business Continuity Programs," and it may become the industry standard for all organizations, including governments and businesses.

The standard was endorsed by the 9/11 Commission. This encyclopedic document has been reviewed by countless experts, and the result is quite thorough. It can be a useful document or checklist for middle managers. By itself, however, it is not a panacea, for several reasons.

As Joseph D. Whitley, the former general counsel to the Department of Homeland Security, put it: "NFPA 1600 is an important first step. However, it is only a first step: NFPA 1600 is a generic document that provides guidance at thirty thousand feet."

Moving closer to 100 percent preparedness will require organizations to implement the general features of NFPA 1600, but to drill down much deeper. Tying this to incentives to encourage such positive behavior is a useful approach. Nonetheless, we have also seen an upsurge in preparedness that is the result of regulation. Most recently, Congress has required the Department of Homeland Security to create national standards to enhance security at the nation's most at-risk chemical facilities

Given the growing distaste for bureaucracy, the NFPA 1600—which looks like, feels like, and reads like a government manual—needs to be made user-friendly if it is to succeed at all.

This document or similar efforts could be part of the proposed International Crisis Management Institute discussed in this chapter. By itself, however, it is another bureaucratic standard.

Crisis Readiness Is a Governance Issue

"We've now entered a wake-up call period, where boards are looking around and saying 'it could happen to us.' In fact, it is astonishing to me to see the movement among board members regarding crisis management." (Suzanne Hopgood, interview with the author)

"Effective crisis management, including planning for and responding to crisis, depends on an honest and courageous chief executive who is willing to meet challenges head-on, and a board that is willing to ask questions, take action, and even take charge when needed. Even more fundamentally, a corporation's response to risk and potential crisis depends on a strong foundation of corporate governance." (Report of the NACD Blue Ribbon Commission on Risk Oversight)

"[E]nsuring that sound crisis response planning is done by management is one of the essential functions of the board. The board's oversight responsibility is generally well understood in areas such as strategy, budgeting, capital transactions, acquisitions, and CEO succession. It is equally the board's responsibility to see that crisis response planning receives the appropriate emphasis among the many issues competing for the attention of the board and management. There is a broad range of possible action by a company in the area of crisis response planning—the board's judgment on how much is appropriate should be expressly brought to bear on this question. It is too important to leave to management without board oversight." (Suzanne Hopgood and Michael Tankersley, "Is My Company Really Ready for a Crisis?," *Corporate Board Member*, April 12, 2006)

"Now the heat on directors is growing more intense. Their reputations are increasingly at risk when the companies they watch over are tainted by scandal. Their judgment is being questioned by activist shareholders outraged by sky-high pay packages. And investors and regulators are subjecting their actions to higher scrutiny. Long gone are the days when a director could get away with a quick rubber-stamp of a CEO's plans.

"The old rules of civility that discouraged directors from asking managers tough or embarrassing questions are eroding. At the same time, board members are being forced to devote more time and energy to many of their most important duties: setting CEO compensation, overseeing the auditing of financial statements, and, when needed, investigating crises. That's the good news. The bad news is they are so busy delving into the minutiae of compliance that they don't have nearly as much time to advise corporate chieftains on strategy.

"The increased scrutiny on boards means that a perfunctory review will not suffice if a scandal strikes. Directors can no longer afford to defer to management in a crisis. They must roll up their sleeves and move into watchdog mode." (Nanette Byrnes and Jane Sasseen, "Board of Hard Knocks," *Business Week*, January 22, 2007)

The National Association of Corporate Directors' Blue Ribbon Commission on Risk Oversight states, "If true reform is to occur, directors must be a permanent and active part of the solution. Above all, the commission statement continues, "Risk oversight must be a priority for all boards, especially in turbulent times."

Oversight, according to the NACD, refers to the exercise of the director's fiduciary duty of care on behalf of the owners, and by extension, other stakeholders in the corporation. Under normal circumstances, boards have a primary fiduciary duty to shareholders. Indeed, so-called "agency theory," a frequent topic in the academic literature on corporate governance, says that managers are merely the agents of stockholders, whose money they are handling. And that directors are there to make sure that manager-agents act properly. (Report of the NACD Blue Ribbon Commission on Risk Oversight, 2002, 2003, 2006)

Suzanne Hopgood and Michael Tankersley (also authors of *Board Leadership for the Company in Crisis*, National Association of Corporate Directors, 2005), raise the direct question: "Who is responsible for assuring that a company is well prepared to meet the crises of 2006 and beyond?"

Their answer: "The board. This is not to say that management's role is not critical to an effective crisis planning and response process, or that the CEO should not be taking the lead. The primary task of a company's leaders, according to Peter Drucker, is 'to make sure of the institution's capacity for survival—to make sure of its structural strength and soundness, of its capacity to survive a blow, and to adapt to sudden change.' It is much too important," they emphasize, "to leave to management without board oversight." (Hopgood and Tankersley, "Is My Company Really Ready for a Crisis?")

Hopgood and Tankersley point to ". . . six compelling reasons why directors should insist that management and board attention be focused on crisis response planning:

"Even limited planning will help the company to avoid common blunders, particularly in managing communications, that turn manageable crises into disasters.

"Planning will decrease the number of decisions that must be made in the early stages of a crisis and allow more attention to those that remain, improving the quality of decision-making.

"Organizing the company's crisis response team in advance will allow the necessary expertise to be assembled quickly and begin working immediately when a crisis hits. Good outside advisors are not easy to find; planning will help assure they are available when needed.

"Many crises begin as manageable problems that then escalate to disastrous proportion. Focused crisis planning makes it more likely that potential crises will be contained before they escalate.

"Directors are obligated to use ordinary care in their decision-making and oversight of the company. Ordinarily careful and prudent individuals buy insurance and make plans to weather personal disasters. Companies should engage in crisis response planning for the same reasons.

"While the prospect of directors encountering personal liability for failing to engage in crisis planning is generally remote, when a crisis does arrive, ill-advised responses of the board, management, and employees can create liability for individuals and the organization. Crisis planning will identify these risks and how to avoid them."

The addition of a board-level crisis preparedness committee, charged with overseeing their company's crisis preparedness, will require several steps:

- Basic understanding of risk management and risk communication.
- Benchmarking or guidance to determine what an effective plan is. A number of benchmarks exist, including The Business Roundtable's Post-9/11 Crisis Communications Tool Kit, and the NFPA 1600 guidance.
- Incentives that can be tied directly to CEO compensation. It seems mundane but simple: Hold CEOs accountable for the clarity and completeness of their plans, scheduling for training and simulations, etc. These are easily documented accomplishments, and their importance is of such vital nature that a CEO who avoids these obligations should be penalized where it hurts—in his checkbook.
- Continued awareness and briefings for new directors, such as those the NACD now conducts for hundreds of new directors, which are a major step toward creating accountability.

Specifically, boards can begin the accountability process by implementing the following steps:

- Demanding to see the existing crisis plans
- Authorizing budget expenditures for crisis planning
- Asking tough questions, such as: Where is all this cash coming from? Where did the company's cash go?
- Determining if there are any lapses in ethics
- Ensuring the company has identified in the most direct way (i.e., without probability weighting) all possible crises. And if any of these were to occur, that the company is ready to respond. And if not, why? And what will it take to be ready?
- Being ready to step in quickly in the worst-case situation where senior management may be implicated in a crisis and not be able to function As Jack and Suzy Welch put it: "[T]he board must assess and challenge management. It must get out of headquarters to see if employees in the field are really carrying out the mission and hewing it to the values that the brass espouses in the boardroom. But ultimately, a board and management must play on the same team, not operate at cross-purposes." (Jack and Suzy Welch, "Ideas The Welch Way," *Business Week*, December 25, 2006/January 1, 2007)

Boards will need credible, generally accepted guidelines. The National Association of Corporate Directors' Board Leadership for the Company in Crisis and The Business Roundtable's Post-9/11 Crisis

Communication Tool Kit are important resources for board members. Books and websites are filled with ideas for the ground rules for crisis planning. The problem is that no one set of ideas has risen to the surface as the generally accepted guideline for best practice.

Shareholder Activism Is Coming of Age

I recall having the outspoken Evelyn Y. Davis on my Washington TV program in the 1970s. Davis, who owned one share of stock in lots of Fortune 500s, made a career of being the annoying but often accurate gadfly at annual meetings. She was outspoken but essentially alone. While she attracted lots attention from the media, she made few inroads because she had no constituency or support.

Then came Ralph Nader and unions, religious organizations, and others, who bought a few shares, giving them the platform for urging environmental and social changes.

Over the past several years, shareholder activism has risen to a more sophisticated art, with major investment funds attracting attention with resolutions on a variety of issues. Make no mistake—the activists have the resources to mount campaigns, use the media, create blogs, and create support. The years 2006 and 2007 were watershed years for shareholder activism. First came the ouster, after shareholder pressure, of the chief executives at Pfizer and Sovereign Bank. Then Ralph V. Whitworth—who had helped found the United Shareholders Association in 1986, and had selected about fifty companies a year to be the subject of embarrassing questions—applied the final pressure to unseat The Home Depot's chairman, Robert Nardelli, for his large compensation package and deteriorating share price. Whitworth, whose fund owns a 1.2 percent stake in The Home Depot, may yet win a board seat as well. And, observers say, The Home Depot is but the beginning.

"Activist shareholders have a power and audience beyond what they've ever enjoyed," said Howard Steinberg, a lawyer who advises corporate boards and deal-makers. "They're developing a credible track record, and as a result, more and more managers are forced to engage with them. Activists' time has come." (Charles Duhigg, "Disgruntled Investors Get Spot in Center Ring," *San Diego Union-Tribune*, January 5, 2007)

While compensation is the primary concern of shareholder activists, and it is gaining steam, it is reasonable to expect that another topic on their list can and should be crisis readiness. This is a logical step, because there is clear evidence that a poorly handled crisis, especially by a company with a stale plan or no plan at all, risks reputational disaster—with a resulting decline in share price.

Shareholder pressure may not always be played out in the headlines, but it is there. As John Wilcox, head of corporate governance at the giant TIAA-CREF fund, said, "Our strategy in the activist area is to meet one-on-one with managements. Quiet diplomacy is the way we work."(Jeff Nash, "The Payparazzi," *Financial Week*, January 15, 2007)

While pressure mounts from the new activists, the traditional boycott is still alive. Boycotts are part of our history. Though their results have been uneven, they are with us and should not be ignored. While the vast numbers of boycotts are annoyances and embarrassments to companies, with little affect on sales, some have made deep and lasting inroads.

The most successful boycott in American history was the Boston Tea Party in 1773, staged to rebel against taxation without representation. The Montgomery Bus Boycott of 1955, after Rosa Parks was arrested for refusing to move to the back of the bus, was a success for civil rights.

Several years ago, People for the Ethical Treatment of Animals waged an unrelenting, often invasive campaign against the killing of animals for fur coats. Countless consumers quickly stopped wearing their fur coats in public, for fear they would be splashed with paint by the PETA pickets. And many more stopped buying fur coats, forcing the closing of many shops. Several years later, the industry has slowly rebounded. But some retailers are gone forever. Though less violent, PETA's boycott campaign against the cosmetic companies forced the end of most animal testing.

Today's boycotters have far more tools available to them than the citizens of 1773 Boston did. The web has had an enormous impact, giving activists the means, for little or no cost, to share information, ideas and plans, and to speak out on blogs and other sites.

Other boycotts go on for years and never seem to go away. One such boycott is the movement to ban so-called bioengineered "Frankenfoods." I was a consultant for two of the annual scientific meetings of the Biotechnology Industry Organization. With more than ten thousand scientists coming together for several days, there was concern about the effects of protesters outside the convention halls. While they were not able to block entrance to the halls, as they intended, they did attract a great deal of media attention because of their colorful parades and loud protest statements. They still are a force, perhaps in large part because they raised fears of many food products that have not yet materialized.

Other boycotts are desperate efforts for well-intentioned causes that simply go nowhere. But they all stir corporate anxiety. Several years ago, when the French were testing nuclear weapons on remote Pacific islands, protesters threatened French consumer products companies with boycotts if they did not lobby the government to stop the testing. The strategy did not work. The companies did not want to become involved in the issue, and the actual boycotts faded quickly. And the boycott of Exxon gas stations in protest against the Exxon Valdez crisis lingered for years, while Exxon's profits soared.

Whether you are faced with a boycott, with pickets and blogs, or shareholder pressure, the strategy for the company should be the same: Find out as much as you can about the protesters and their claims. Meet with them. During these discussions, determine the legitimacy of the issue and what it might take to come to terms. In most cases it will be a long process, but it should begin.

Part III

The Tool Kit

8: Tools You Can Use: A Guide to Commonly Used Terms

The crises of the past few years and the creation of the Department of Homeland Security have spawned a new vocabulary, with acronyms and shorthand. Following is a guide to some of the more commonly used terms.

Blogs

According to Wikipedia.org, a blog (short for web log) is "a web page that serves as a publicly-accessible personal journal for an individual. Typically updated daily, blogs often reflect the personality of the author."

The definition of blog is constantly evolving, though, as blogs move into the mainstream, shedding their image as the bastion of the self-obsessed who just have to self-express. Thousands of new blogs are being created every day, for all sorts of purposes. Rather than existing only to catalog someone's personal life, many blogs serve as discussion communities about particular issues.

Bridging

The interview technique that calls for the person answering a question to hold the moment after answering the question, and emphasize a different—though related—point by using such bridging phrases as, "But the important point to note is . . .," or, "Let me also point out that . . ."

Business Continuity

The processes and procedures an organization puts in place to assure that essential functions can continue during and after a disaster.

Call Tree

A structured process that allows members of the crisis team to be contacted rapidly—either by a series of personal calls or by an automated system.

Dirty Bomb

A crude method for spreading radiation over a substantial area. A dirty bomb does not create a nuclear blast. It is made by packing dynamite or other conventional explosive with any type of radioactive material—e.g., isotopes used in X-ray machines—and, when detonated, it spreads the radioactive material.

GETS Cards

Government Emergency Telecommunications Service (GETS) cards, which provide priority telephone connectivity during an emergency to parties considered by the federal government to have a role in addressing issues related to homeland security.

Incident Commander

A government official in charge of coordinating resources and strategies in the event of an emergency.

Incident of National Significance (INS)

An actual or potential high-impact event that requires immediate and extensive coordination of federal government resources to save lives and minimize damage.

International Standards Organization (ISO)

A network of the national standards institutes of 157 countries, on the basis of one member per country, with a Central Secretariat in Geneva, Switzerland, that coordinates the system. The ISO is a non-governmental organization; its members are not, as in the case of the United Nations, delegations of national governments. Nevertheless, the ISO occupies a special position between the public and private sectors. Many of its member institutes are part of the governmental structure of their countries, or are mandated by their government. Other members have their roots uniquely in the private sector, having been set up by national partnerships of industry associations. Therefore, the ISO is able to act as a bridging organization in which a consensus can be reached on solutions that meet both the requirements of business and the broader needs of society, such as the needs of stakeholder groups like consumers and users.

Interoperability

The ability of first-response agencies (fire, police, emergency medical services) to communicate with each other during an emergency or disaster.

ISACs

Information sharing and analysis centers, which are associated with each of the major economic sectors, including communications, electricity, finance, transportation, information technology, public transit, and water. The ISACs provide a framework for sharing physical- and cyber-security information.

Joint Field Office (JFO)

A temporary federal facility established locally to provide a central point for federal, state, and local executives with responsibility for incident direction and operations.

National Incident Management System (NIMS)

A Department of Homeland Security plan developed so that responders from different jurisdictions and disciplines can work together to deal with natural disasters and emergencies, including acts of terrorism. The plan includes a unified approach to incident management, standard command and management structures, and emphasis on preparedness, mutual aid, and resource management. The NIMS Integration Center (NIC) oversees all aspects of the NIMS, including the development of compliance criteria and implementation activities at federal, state, and local levels. It provides guidance and support to jurisdictions and incident management and responder organizations as they adopt the system.

National Infrastructure Protection Plan (NIPP)

A Department of Homeland Security plan that provides a coordinated approach to critical infrastructure and key resource protection roles and responsibilities for federal, state, local, tribal, and private-sector security partners. The NIPP sets national priorities, goals, and requirements for effective distribution of funding and resources that will help ensure that the government, economy, and public services continue in the event of a terrorist attack or other disaster.

National Response Plan (NRP)

The National Response Plan establishes a comprehensive, all-hazards approach to managing domestic incidents. The plan forms the basis of how the federal government coordinates with state, local, and tribal governments, and with the private sector, during incidents.

NFPA 1600

A detailed checklist of suggested crisis planning requirements, created for the American National Standards Institute by the National Fire Protection Association.

Patriot Act

Acronym for the U.S. law: Provide Appropriate Tools Required to Intercept and Obstruct Terrorism.

PS-Prep

FEMA's voluntary crisis planning accreditation program, based on NFPA 1600

Ready.gov

A national Department of Homeland Security public service campaign designed to educate Americans to prepare for and respond to emergencies, including natural disasters and threat of terrorist attacks. The series includes components for the home, children, and business.

Risk communication

A specialized area of communication that is based on well-researched guidelines for communicating risk information to the public.

Shelter in Place

Staying in the building you are in, if it is habitable, in the event of an emergency involving air contamination.

Terrorist Threat Integration Center (TTIC)

A unit of the Department of Homeland Security responsible for gathering and analyzing threat information from across the entire federal government. The TTIC is based at the Central Intelligence Agency (CIA).

TOPOFF

Part of the national terrorism response exercise program, TOPOFF is a congressionally mandated exercise program designed to test and strengthen local, state, and federal government resources.

9: A Standard Approach to Crisis Planning

This chapter presents a standard approach to crisis planning for board members and senior management, based on collective experiences and best practices. While there is no one-size-fits-all approach, there is some common ground that all can use as a foundation.

Checklists for the Board and Key Crisis Team Members

Increasingly, crisis team members and board members look to checklists to remind them of the basics of crisis readiness and response. Following are suggested checklists for key functions:

Board
Pre-Crisis:
Ask questions:
Where is the plan?
Is there a plan?
When was it last updated?
What are the top ten risks for the company?
Are you prepared to face them if they occur?
In Crisis
How can we help?

CEO
Pre-Crisis
Ask questions:
Where is my copy of the plan?
Have we implemented suggestions from the last simulation or actual crisis?

Have we scheduled the next simulation? When?

What should I worry about?

Is the new plan ready as an app on my iPad?

What are the latest surveys telling us about crisis trends?

In Crisis

Chair the crisis team

Serve as chief spokesperson to the public/media, customers, employees, Wall Street

Keep employee morale a top priority

Ask the tough questions

Listen, decide, criticize, praise

VP Communications and Team

Pre Crisis

Keep the company crisis-ready:

Update the plan

Keep key contacts up to date

Practice the notification system

Identify and train all spokespersons and alternates

Monitor media and social media for early warnings and trends

In Crisis

Activate the crisis team

Activate the crisis room

Create key messages

Create FAQs

Get the news out quickly and steadily

Monitor media and social media

Monitor stock price

Change the website when needed

Respond to media calls

Organize press conference

Coordinate international response

VP Legal and Team

In Crisis

Organize investigation of legal aspects of crisis

Work closely with communications to approve press releases *fast.*

When it's all over pull together the debrief of lessons learned.

Liaison with regulatory or legislative contacts

VP Marketing/Sales and Team
In Crisis
Activate customer hot line
Notify key customers
Suspend advertising or events
Activate customer research

VP Operations and Team
In Crisis
Activate rescue logistics
Activate facilities restoration
Activate business continuity
Assure that all nonaffected aspects of the business continue as
 normal

VP Security and Team
In Crisis
Keep all locations notified of situation
Provide extra security when needed
Work with local, state, and federal law enforcement

The Top Things You Need to Do to Be Crisis-Ready

- Conduct an annual checkup to see where you fit on the readiness scale.
- Have a plan, and keep it simple and up to date.
- Make crisis preparation a full-time commitment.
- Think prevention.
- Have a backup for everything—from people to infrastructure.
- Remember your employees and their families.
- Keep your suppliers and customers aware of your plans.
- Be ready to explain risks to the public in a sensitive, open manner.
- Practice according to a schedule—and stick to it.
- Don't hide—don't even consider it.
- And remember the basics:

     —Have crisis and security executives report directly to the
     CEO.
     —Keep the plan simple.
     —Practice, practice, practice.

Helping the Board Get Started

The first and most important step for any company is the creation
of the permanent crisis governance committee of the board. This concept
should become standard for all companies, assuring that crisis readiness is
a required, standard operating procedure.

This will not happen overnight, but the time has come to begin.
And the first step is the creation of a crisis governance committee.

Once a crisis governance committee has been formed, the first step
for the committee should be a review of the company's crisis procedures. The
score-based tool presented below is offered as a means for reviewing the
company's crisis plan.

The crisis governance committee of the board should have specific
oversight over the company's crisis preparedness plans and monitor the
plan's status, relevance, and utility. Should a crisis occur, the governance
committee would be available for counsel, but would not be involved in the
day-to-day and hour-by-hour management of the crisis. However, should
the CEO or other senior officers of the company be unavailable or otherwise
not appropriate for involvement in the crisis response, the board should
immediately step in to assume management of the crisis.

A final step, and an equally important one, is the board's review of
the lessons learned from any drill or actual crisis, with assurance that steps
will be taken for continuous improvement based on those lessons learned.

The Plan

In the months following the Tylenol tamperings, as we worked to
define the parameters for crisis preparedness, the trend was toward creation
of large manuals. These gradually gave way to shorter, user-friendly manuals
of less than forty pages. They were still too long to be useful during a crisis,
though they had an important place during training. The state of the art
today includes the crisis manual—preferably called the crisis resource

manual—and a pocket card that lists key contact information and checklists reminding the team members of their duties.

Crisis Plan Diagnosis

We are a nation of scorekeepers. We have scores for football, cholesterol, and IQs. The time has come for a crisis-readiness score that can graphically highlight a company's readiness. Companies of all sizes and in all industries face common crisis-readiness challenges. The following tool will help appraise any company's readiness:

Score each item on a scale of 1 to 3, with 3 being the best. Looking at the score for each item and the average for the total will give you a clear—perhaps startling —picture of where the company stands.

The scale is based on the following:

1—Unacceptable

2—Marginal, still needs improvement

3—Acceptable

Score

(1) Does a crisis plan exist?

(2) Is there a pocket card or smartphone app version of the plan?

(3) Has the plan been updated in the past three months?

(4) Is there a dedicated situation room?

(5) Can an existing conference room quickly be converted into a situation room?

(6) Is the CEO directly involved in crisis planning?

(7) Has the CEO been briefed on the company's crisis plan within the past thirty days?

(8) Is the CEO the chair of the crisis team?

(9) Is the crisis team membership clearly defined?

(10) Is the responsibility for crisis readiness a full-time staff function?

(11) Has the company identified all potential risks without regard for their probability?

(12) Has the following been asked regarding each risk:

A. If this happened today, how well equipped would we be to handle it?

B. Has everything reasonable been done to reduce or eliminate this risk?

(13) If a crisis occurred in the company today, could the crisis team come together within thirty minutes?

(14) If the primary team members are not available, are designated backups available?

(15) Can the plan pass a "contact test"? Specifically, assuming the plan contains contact information for the crisis team and you placed calls to six team members on their home or cell phones, would you reach them after hours?

(16) Is there a procedure for regularly verifying contact information?

(17) Do your headquarters and branch operations know all there is to know about local emergency resources—governmental and non-governmental?

(18) Are crisis simulations conducted at least semiannually?

(19) Once these simulations have been scheduled, are they considered firm commitments? Or are they postponed frequently?

(20) Is there a protocol for follow-through on the lessons learned and changes that should be made to the plan?

(21) Are newly appointed members of the crisis team trained to understand their responsibilities?

(22) Is there a regular schedule for evacuation drills?

(23) Are the evacuation drills successively challenging? Or are they the same old ones, i.e., "Go to the nearest exit, descend the stairs, and wait until the all-clear is sounded"?

(24) Are emergency personal supplies such as flashlights on hand for all employees during an evacuation?

(25) Do you have a business continuity plan?

(26) Has it been tested?

10: The Insider's Secrets to Good Crisis Planning

"It's better to have the plan and not need it, than to need the plan and not have it."
    —*Anonymous*

The War Room

The crisis room, command center, or war room, as it is sometimes called, is one of the most important details. The crisis team needs a place to work. It can be a simple conference room used for everyday purposes but immediately available in a crisis. Or it can be elaborate. Airlines have some of the better-developed crisis command centers. At American Airlines, the strategic command center is a vast room featuring a large, horseshoe-shaped table with fully equipped work stations and a conference call line that can accommodate as many as two hundred outside callers. Large-screen television monitors set up to receive satellite broadcasts allow command center employees to monitor all news coverage of the crisis. (Paul Argenti, *Harvard Business Review*, December 1, 2002)

Minimum Requirements for a Functioning Crisis Room:
- Phone and laptop ports at each seat
- Multidirectional speaker phone
- TV monitors, maps, and whiteboards on the walls
- Copier, printer, and fax
- Easels with flip chart

And make certain that, in the event of a crisis:
- You have access to cash
- The company can handle a barrage of phone calls from the media, customers, and suppliers (assuming the phones are working)
- The company's travel agent has access to charter flight operators if you need to send a team to a crisis site.

Smart companies have learned that a crisis cannot be managed in an ordinary conference room. For companies with extensive operations, the crisis center becomes Mission Control. Look, for example, at FedEx Emergency Central, as described on CNN:

Supplies are a critical requirement. Don't leave them to chance. FEMA reminds businesses of some of the basics to have on hand:

• Battery-powered radios, and a special radio that can receive weather alerts from the National Oceanographic and Atmospheric Administration (NOAA).

• Copies of important records such as site maps, building plans, insurance polices, employee contact information, supplier and shipper contact lists, computer backups, law enforcement contacts, and other priority documents in hard copy in a waterproof, fireproof container; with a backup at a continuity site.

Recommended supplies for employees:

• Water—one gallon of water per person for drinking and sanitation
• Food—at least a three-day supply of non-perishable food
• Flashlight and extra batteries
• First-aid kit and three-day supply of prescription or other medications
• Whistle to signal for help
• Dust mask or cotton T-shirt to help filter the air
• Moist towelettes
• Can opener
• Sturdy shoes, extra clothes, and blankets
• Cash

(CNN broadcast, October 3, 2005)

Keep Your Contact Information Connected

Even the best plans may fall apart if the system for notifying crisis team members and other key staff at the onset of a crisis fails. Despite automation, updating many notification systems—e.g., phone numbers—remain a manual process, dependent on periodic checks or reminders to let the keeper of the data know of new mobile and home numbers. The solution is a simple one: Connect the crisis plan to all the other inputs—e.g., human resources records linked to the plan, so that changes click in when they are made.

Consider All Risks

Forget probability tables. If anyone had considered the possibility of two passenger planes being deliberately flown into the World Trade Center, it would have been so low on the probability scale that the right questions would never have been asked. Well, it did happen, and the improbable and impossible may happen again. Or consider the near-sinking of a mammoth cruise ship. Well, it did happen.

It is not impossible to imagine the extreme situations. While you will never define them all, a free-thinking meeting of departments defining the predictable and extreme scenarios will yield a manageable list, to which you should then ask all the "What if?" questions—specifically:
- If this happened, would we be prepared to face it?
- What needs to be done to prepare?
- Can we prevent this?
- Are we fostering open communication to prevent a crisis?

The Headquarters Crisis Plan is not Enough

Each location and operation of the company should have its own crisis plan, modeled after the home office crisis plan but tailored to the needs of the location and operation. This is especially important given the increasing number of offshore operations. In order to facilitate the creation of the localized crisis plans, it is useful to provide each location with a tool kit or template for the creation of their crisis plan.

Crisis Teams—The Who and the How

Organization patterns for crisis teams vary. In many corporations— especially those with high-risk or regulated businesses such as transportation or chemicals—the leaders in the crisis function tend to be in the security, or health and safety departments. In other, seemingly less crisis-prone, companies, they may be in corporate communications. In reality, the most reasonable answer is a partnership among the three functions—security, health and safety, and communications. In some of the largest corporations, the CEO may never become involved in a crisis unless and until it reaches huge proportions. In others, the CEO is immediately informed and may lead the crisis team.

Well-defined crisis teams are essential elements of a crisis plan. The most effective structure is a simple one, consisting of:

The senior crisis team, chaired by the CEO. In many companies it also is appropriate to create brand-specific crisis teams, headed by the brand CEOs. In both cases, the team members typically include the senior executives for communications, human resources, legal, operations or manufacturing, information technology, customer service, and sales and marketing.

The crisis evaluation team, which may be activated to determine whether an early warning or rumors may be an actual crisis about to occur or not.

The crisis support teams, which include a defined number of support staff for each area, charged with carrying out the decisions of the senior crisis team.

Go teams, comprised of trained volunteers from mid-management ranks who can be sent to the site of a serious incident to offer support and logistical assistance to customers and employees.

Employee emergency team, charged with tracking, communicating with, and caring for the needs of employees in a serious incident in which employees may have lost their homes, or may be required to work at off-site locations because their work locations may have been adversely affected.

Business continuity team, whose function is to plan and implement the company's continuity plan in the aftermath of an incident that may have shut down one or more facilities.

Business Continuity Planning

Business continuity, once the sleepy function that few cared about, has become an urgent concern, since the events of 9/11. In 2004, the SEC approved the NYSE and NASD's proposed requirements for listed companies' business continuity obligations:

NYSE Rule 446 and NASD Rules 3510 and 3520 outline a set of ten minimum requirements that must be addressed, regardless of the size of the member company:

Ten Minimum Compliance Elements

(1) Books and records backup and recovery (hard copy and electronic).

(2) Identification of all mission-critical systems and backup for such systems

(3) Financial and operational risk assessments

(4) Alternate communications between customers and the firm

(5) Alternate communications between the firm and its employees

(6) Alternate physical location of employees

(7) Critical business constituent, bank and counter-party activity

(8) Regulatory reporting

(9) Communications with regulators

(10) Method of assuring customers prompt access to their funds and securities in the event the member or member organization determines it is unable to continue its business

There is now a significant amount of professional activity taking place in this specialty, and virtually everything current can be found in the free weekly online newsletter, Continuity Central, published in London. Highly recommended! (*www.continuitycentral.com*)

How quickly your company can get back to business after a terrorist attack, tornado, fire, or flood often depends on emergency planning done today. Start planning now to improve the likelihood that your company will survive and recover.

The Department of Homeland Security provides a useful overview of business continuity planning:

• Carefully assess how your company functions, both internally and externally, to determine which staff, materials, procedures and equipment are absolutely necessary to keep the business operating.

• Review your business process flow chart, if one exists.

• Identify operations critical to survival and recovery.

• Include emergency payroll, expedited financial decision-making, and accounting systems to track and document costs in the event of a disaster.

• Establish procedures for management succession. Consider Including at least one person who is not at the company headquarters, if applicable.

- Identify your suppliers, shippers, resources, and other businesses you must interact with on a daily basis.
- Develop professional relationships with more than one company to use in case your primary contractor cannot service your needs. A disaster that shuts down a key supplier can be devastating to your business.
- Create a contact list for existing critical business contractors and others you plan to use in an emergency. Keep this list with other important documents on file, in your emergency supply kit, and at an off-site location.
- Plan what you will do if your building, plant, or store is not accessible. This type of planning is often referred to as a continuity of operations plan, or COOP, and includes all facets of your business.
- Consider if you can run the business from a different location or from your home.
- Develop relationships with other companies to use their facilities in case a disaster makes your location unusable.
- Plan for payroll continuity.
- Decide who should participate in putting together your emergency plan.
- Include workers from all levels—both in planning and as active members of the emergency management team.
- Consider a broad cross section of people from throughout your organization, but focus on those with expertise vital to daily business functions. These will likely include people with technical skills as well as managers and executives.
- Define crisis management procedures and individual responsibilities in advance.
- Make sure those involved know what they are supposed to do.
- Train others in case you need backup help.
- Coordinate with others.
- Meet with other businesses in your building or industrial complex.
- Talk with first responders, emergency managers, community organizations, and utility providers.
- Plan with your suppliers, shippers, and others you regularly do business with.
- Share your plans and encourage other businesses to set in motion their own continuity planning and offer to help others.

• Review your emergency plans annually. Just as your business changes over time, so do your preparedness needs. When you hire new employees or when there are changes in how your company functions, you should update your plans and inform your people.

(United States Department of Homeland Security)

11: Validating the Crisis and Continuity Plans to Keep Them Alive

Even the best-looking plan is dead on arrival if it is simply filed away for the day it may be needed. A crisis plan is a living document that should be used for training, simulating, and briefing new employees and crisis team members. Anything short of that is ineffective.

Don't forget the small stuff

While an entire book could be devoted to details of crisis preparedness, we mention details here because lack of attention to small details could hamper or shut down a crisis response, or severely hamper it.
Consider some of the small stuff:
• Do enough people have the right phones?
• Do they have spare batteries and power chargers?
• Does everyone have the right ID to give them access to what may become restricted areas?

Practice Makes Almost Perfect

How do you decide on and conduct the training and drills that work—with tips for crisis prevention and continuous improvement?
A number of formats are available for simulations. And some of the best are the simplest and shortest. In each case, a maximum of two staff members should be designated in advance as the "trusted agents" who design the scenario in strict confidence. The most effective scenario is one that:

- Has never occurred at the company
- Is based on one of the known risks the company faces
- Is clearly described and is challenging
- May have occurred at some other company

Tabletop Exercise (time commitment: two hours)

The advantage of this format, which is conducted around a conference table, is that it is informal. The team is given a scenario, and team members are asked to provide their action plans in line with their responsibilities. This is a good refresher for experienced teams, and provides an opportunity to discuss new vulnerabilities.

Simulated Press Conference (time commitment: one hour)

This exercise, best combined with a half-day crisis training session, is based on a scenario posed to the team. Once the team is given the scenario, they are given time to develop a strategy for solutions and key communications messages that would be conveyed during the mock press conference.

During this time they also choose the spokesperson for the group. It may be the senior executive or another, depending on the situation and their judgment of who will be the best and most appropriate person for the job. They are encouraged to rehearse informally before facing the simulated press conference. For the simulation, facilitators, trainers, and other staff are generally recruited to play the media and ask the tough questions. The event is recorded on video and then played back for critique. When time permits, a second round is conducted, with either an escalation of the original scenario or a new scenario.

Full Simulation (time commitment: four hours)

This is a full test for the team and any support they may call upon within the organization. Ideally, this should be an unannounced event, testing the immediate response of the senior crisis team and the availability of alternates if needed. The simulation begins with a phone call to the duty officer or crisis team chair, in which an employee, reporter, government official, or other source announces a problem that would call for an immediate response. Using a set of "rules of engagement," the team then begins to work together as if the problem were actually occurring. A drill controller is present in the room, periodically giving the team additional details and developments.

An effective simulation also includes a press conference at some point.

During the exercise, the team is allowed to call upon any resources in the company, provided that every call, fax, or e-mail is prefaced by, and ends with, the phrase: *This is a drill.* This format is the most effective and ideally should be conducted twice a year.

The Secrets to Media Success

The First Minutes and Hours

If your crisis is already being covered on TV and online, this is the time to join the media. Like it or not, this critical first hour is your chance to establish your credibility. If you do not, CNN and the others will look for "experts" to fill the void and begin commenting and speculating on what has gone wrong. Usually they are wrong. Waiting too long while the others talk about you will create a bigger problem in the long run, as you try and catch up when you can. Social media have changed the rules of the game.

You do not need to say very much in this first hour. Great if you can, but you often do not have enough facts. A simple acknowledgement of the crisis: "Such and such has happened at location X. Rescue teams are on the scene. We do not have any details at this time. Our first priority is rescuing the people inside." Simple? It works. It's true. It shows you care and are dealing with the problem. It also shows you're not hiding.

So you are in the midst of a crisis, and your company is besieged with media representatives who want to know what happened, who's been hurt or killed, what damage has been done, and what's being done about it.

These are simple questions with often complex answers that need to be put in context so that the reporter, often lacking expertise in your company or industry, can understand all this and get the story straight.

They Have a Job to Do, and So Do You

Any media briefing or interview is pointless unless you have a message.

Experiences in a variety of situations have shown that any audience—your employees, or the general public, for example—will absorb an average of three messages at any one time. The basic message, research has shown, is most effective when it can be delivered in twenty-seven words. And in a crisis, the best messages are ones that show compassion, especially if there have been injuries or deaths; a commitment to solve the crisis; and an explanation of the actions underway.

In crafting these messages, it is very important to give life (in addition to the basic twenty-seven words)—to prove them, with illustrations, simple statistics, or an anecdote. In the best of situations, your messages and their proofs become quotable for the media—traditional and social. Long-winded messages will bore the media and stand little chance of reaching the public. Shorter messages will attract their attention. Think about a message that, with its proof, runs less than a minute. And, in a tweet, 140 characters.

The difficulty many spokespersons face is making certain they get their messages across. What, you ask, do I do if the reporter or an audience of employees never asks the right question that fits my messages?

Answer the questions. But look for the first moment when you can say, "But I would also like to point out . . .," or, "The real issue here is . . .," and give your most important message. Look for other openings when you can give the other messages. The reporter will let you do it—after all, you are making news. This technique, called bridging, is simple. The tough part is to remember to do it.

What Can I Do to Overcome Stage Fright?

First, forget that oft-quoted "research" that shows that people would rather die than get up and give a speech or face the media. It is utter nonsense. But stage fright is real. It also can be overcome.

Remember:

- You know more than the audience.

• Most audiences want to hear what you have to say. Yes, some can be hostile—and we will talk about them in a bit. But most are not.

Now for the practical:

The more you know the subject, and the messages or text, the more comfortable you will be.

You need to own the words. The best presentation, talk, or interview is the one you own—write it, edit it, make the words yours. The words must ring true to you.

Walking onto a stage carrying words someone else has written for you, and that you've not reviewed and rewritten to create ownership, is a sure path to the jitters. If you have a speech writer, great. It's a huge help for a busy schedule. But it's not a panacea. You still need to edit it, change it, and make it yours.

Read it over and over and over—as many as six times. Make changes as you read. It may be a word here and a word there, or it may be whole paragraphs that need fine-tuning. But take the time to do it. And do it the day before. Not an hour before. That's a sure-fire way to create panic and stage fright.

Then relax before the speech. Take time out. I'm reminded of the time a few years ago when I walked into the office of a CEO I had prepared to face an aggressive press conference. We had spent several hours doing role-play, and he was very good, but when I walked into his office an hour before the event, there were a number of executives hovering around his desk, saying things like, "Well, if you don't want to do it, don't do it." I quickly sensed he was getting cold feet, trying to avoid a press event he could not avoid without risking serious embarrassment. I politely asked everyone to leave and closed the door, after which I asked the CEO what his problem was. He replied that even though the preparation had gone well, the reality was daunting for him, since he had never faced an actual aggressive press corps. I told him in no uncertain terms that he was excellent at it, and that he had no choice. I then suggested he go to the company fitness center and go on the treadmill for forty-five minutes—which was something he did every day—and then I would meet him and walk with him to the press conference. He did just that and was terrific under pressure.

Some Tried and True, Essential Rules for Working with the Media

   • Nothing is ever off the record. In today's highly competitive media world, there have been violations of the "off the record" trust. It never was a wise idea to be circumspect, and it is true today. If it is worth saying, it is worth saying on the record. If not, simply do not say it.

   • Avoid saying "No comment." It is quickly perceived as "I'm hiding something." If you cannot comment, at least explain why you cannot. "This is in litigation and for obvious reasons we cannot comment at this point." There. You've explained why, removing the specter of hiding something.

   • Do not criticize the media when speaking to reporters. Strong as the temptation may be, it accomplishes nothing to berate the media for unfair coverage, and it could anger many. It is far more productive to strongly set the record straight, working toward more balanced coverage. Some years ago one of the oil companies, irritated over some stories about the company in the *Wall Street Journal*, made a big announcement that it was canceling all its advertising in the *Journal* because of what it perceived as biased reporting. It did nothing to change the *Journal*'s writing, but the cancellation did create headlines.

   • Insist on background information about the reporters you are to face. While this is not practical for a roomful of reporters you are to face at a press conference, it is practical and useful to know about the reporter you are going to face in a one-on-one interview.

   • Keep eye contact with the reporter. This conveys trust and credibility. When you shift eye contact, you give the impression you are hiding something or are avoiding the question.

   • Do not repeat negatives. For example, if you are asked, "Isn't it true that you fear losing market share if the product is recalled?" and you answer, "No, I do not fear loss of market share, etc., etc.," this gives the reporter quotable material to work with. "Joe Jones, president of the XYZ Company, says he 'does not fear loss of market share.' " If your answer is "No, I cannot speculate, but what I can tell you about the actions we have taken, etc.," you have gone in a positive direction.

   That said, there are no guarantees that the story will please you 100 percent. But the more control you exercise of what you say and how you say it, the greater the chances of balanced writing in the newsroom.

• Be yourself. Do not suddenly take on a new persona for the media. If, for example, you gesture naturally, do so. But if you do not, do not suddenly become a gesturer. It will come across as artificial and distracting.

Understand How to Communicate Risk

Health and safety issues are especially sensitive areas, and you can do more harm than good if you do not follow some of the tested guidelines. Follow the guidelines for communicating with employees and the public, and chances are you can prevent or reduce panic, and offer genuine, life-saving information.

• Listen to the concerns of employees and the public. If you do not listen to them, don't expect them to listen to you. Rapid opinion polls, focus groups, blogs, and other sources of feedback should be used.

• Recognize that people will have many uncertainties—on an emotional as well as a practical or logistical level.

• Be honest, frank, and open. They need to trust you and the others you have chosen as spokespersons. Disclose information in plain and complete terms. Do not hide anything. Communicate quickly and often. Do not speculate. And do not reduce the situation to statistics. People do not want to hear that they may have a one-in-ten chance of dying. They want to know what is being done to help them, and what they can do to help themselves.

• Collaborate with credible experts from universities, government agencies, and health and safety organizations. Two reasons: They can provide useful information, and you can add to your credibility by quoting these recognized and trusted experts. People will respect the expertise you've brought to the table.

• Be honest and open with the media.

• And, above all, speak clearly and with compassion. Express your sympathies up front. People will appreciate it. Use simple, nontechnical language. Use examples when appropriate, but avoid comparisons. Different people react differently to comparisons, and some may become outraged at comparisons that seem to trivialize their fears.

Employees Count

When an explosion rocks a building, a terrorist bomb explodes, or a fire breaks out, employees first want to know that their families are safe and that their families know they are safe. Nothing counts more; smart companies will recognize this and provide the means for employees to communicate—as soon as possible, and before asking them to do anything else.

Concern for employees should be at the top of the crisis response list, for without employees a company does not exist. In order for employees to do their jobs, they need to feel safe, and they need to know from senior management that their safety is a top priority.

As we have seen with the experiences of Katrina, the companies that recovered most quickly were those that had plans for finding their employees and providing housing for them.

A number of steps can be put in place to find employees during a crisis:

• On-site: Set up an electronic system that notes entries and exits, with the ability to create a log of who is in the building and who is not.

• Off-site: Set up a call-in number where any employee—a mile away at a meeting or traveling out of town or overseas—can call and leave an "I'm OK" message.

• Centralize travel arrangements with one agency (or with the company-wide in-house department) so that you can ask for a rapid report on who is traveling and where they are should an emergency hit.

Some Crises Can be Prevented

The best crisis is the one that never happens.

Some crises can be prevented, but it takes organization, determination, and listening skills. Organized prevention programs have the potential for the greatest gain at the least cost, but ironically, it is an area often ignored.

The Crisis Prevention Prescription

Heed early warnings. Katrina and the devastation it caused in the Gulf region are a primary example of warnings ignored. Engineers had warned for years that the region could not withstand a Category 5 hurricane. While the warnings were largely ignored by government agencies, the smart companies in the region planned and practiced for the day.

Take the real crises seriously. One misstep can be excused if you have a strong reserve of good will. Apologize and promise to take steps, and then take them.

Listen to customers. . Many companies ask for customer feedback. The ones who benefit from this feedback are the ones who avoid the next problem. The problem with many feedback mechanisms is that some are simply too time-consuming to complete, and others are too superficial to be of any value.

Think of ways to make the feedback process easy for your customers. Keep the forms short but not superficial. In fact, focus groups can help show the flaws in your feedback system and make it better. Do your customers, for example, have no time to provide anonymous feedback on yes-or-no type forms? Would they prefer a personal call? Would they prefer an online mechanism? Do they want a chance to win a reward for taking part? Would they prefer a charitable contribution made by the company for every completed feedback form?

It's no surprise that customers who volunteer comment are those who have had a bad experience. Watch the blogs. They often will reveal problems by those customers who have little or no confidence in the company feedback mechanisms and are taking the criticism into their own hands.

Listen to employees. Employees—especially those on the front lines of operations and customer service—see and hear firsthand the pulse of the company and its customers. Providing easy ways for them to offer suggestions that can prevent problems and crises can pay back in small and big ways. When employees are encouraged to offer ideas for crisis prevention, they will be forthright and enthusiastic. They will appreciate your efforts when they know they are being heard, and when they are rewarded in some tangible way when their ideas are put into practice. Remember that employees need a variety of ways to provide their ideas—

these may include a special e-mail suggestion box, a write-in address, and a voice-mail box.

Learn from Experience

Whether you've weathered an actual crisis or gone through the rigors of a simulation, one of the most critical steps to take is the debrief— asking everyone involved for their reactions to the experience and the process that guided them. From this debrief, you will inevitably find that changes can be made so you will be better prepared the next time around. You even may discover some procedures that should be changed in order to prevent a crisis from occurring.

In almost all debriefs, lessons surface, revealing steps that can be taken to prevent a crisis. Some of the ideas are small, some large. These lessons may show, for example, that the public address system does not work in all parts of the building, that a security gate is not staffed properly, or that the business continuity site you thought was perfect cannot be reached easily in a huge crush of traffic.

Every lesson and observation, large or small, when followed through, can help prevent a crisis—or least prevent an emergency from escalating to a crisis. Lives may be saved.

The debrief can take many forms. For example, immediately following a simulation, while the entire team is still in the same room, use the opportunity to go around the table and ask everyone individually to give a four-to-five minute rundown of what, in their view, went well and what needs improvement. If their input requires more detail, they should be charged with writing that up immediately after the meeting.

If a crisis has occurred that involved dozens of resources within the company and with outside agencies such as vendors and government agencies, assign someone to conduct interviews with all parties to determine the lessons learned. This, too, should be done immediately.

Finally, if the crisis has involved a small team of perhaps six to eight staff members, a more expedient method would be to ask each to complete a form on which they are asked a number of questions:

(1) Were you notified promptly?

(2) Were you able to reach all the members of the crisis team promptly?

(3) Did you receive a constant flow of information?

(4) Were you able to coordinate with the crisis site so that you could be helpful?

(5) How promptly and thoroughly were media calls handled?

(6) Was media coverage balanced and accurate?

(7) Was a call center set up to handle calls from customers or employees' families? How effective was that effort?

(8) Were the call center personnel trained and equipped to handle the calls?

Travel in the Post-9/11 Era

Business travel has become more complicated since 9/11, and flights are full. There are delays and hassles going through security, occasional evacuations of airports when a suspicious package is found, and the ever-changing rules of what can and cannot be taken aboard a plane.

There are no signs that global business travel is about to disappear, so the smart executives will conduct themselves smartly. This includes but is not limited to the following suggestions:

• Use common sense. Don't go to areas after dark that are known to be unsafe.

• Learn to pack lightly—and carry your bags on.

• Be careful on busy streets. Hold on to your belongings and do not stop to answer questions from passersby–the odds are too great they are looking to catch you off guard and steal your wallet or purse.

• Employees traveling to international destinations present a specific challenge, and experienced business travel departments sign up with one of the international emergency services. They provide country-specific travel advisories, briefings on local business protocols and customs, and emergency aid. Two of the most prominent are International SOS and iJet.

Crises Abroad—What the State Department Does and Does Not Do

Earthquakes, hurricanes, political upheavals, acts of terrorism, and hijackings are only some of the events threatening the safety of Americans abroad. Each event is unique and poses its own special difficulties. However, for the State Department there are certain responsibilities and actions that apply in every disaster or crisis.

When a crisis occurs, the State Department's Bureau of Consular Affairs sets up a task force or working group to bring together all the people necessary to work on that event. Usually this Washington task force will be in touch by telephone twenty-four hours a day with the ambassador and foreign service officers at the embassy in the country affected.

In a task force, the immediate job of the Bureau of Consular Affairs is to respond to the thousands of concerned relatives and friends who begin to telephone the State Department immediately after the news of a disaster is broadcast.

Relatives want information on the welfare of their family members and on the disaster. For hard information, the State Department relies on its embassies and consulates abroad. Often these installations are also affected by the disaster and lack electricity, phone lines, gasoline, etc. Nevertheless, Foreign Service officers work hard to get information back to Washington as quickly as possible. This is rarely as quickly as the press is able to relay information. Foreign Service officers cannot speculate; their information must be accurate. Often this means getting important information from the local government, which may or may not be immediately responsive.

As concerned relatives call in, officers of the Bureau of Consular Affairs collect the names of the Americans possibly involved in the disaster and pass them to the embassy and consulates. Officers at the site attempt to locate these Americans in order to report on their welfare. The officers work with local authorities and, depending on the circumstances, may personally search hotels, airports, hospitals, or even prisons. As they try to get information, their first priority is Americans dead or injured.

Death: When an American dies abroad, the Bureau of Consular Affairs must locate and inform the next of kin. Sometimes this is difficult. If the American's name is known, the Bureau's Office of Passport Services will search for his or her passport application. However, that information may not be current.

The Bureau of Consular Affairs provides guidance to grieving family members on how to make arrangements for local burial or return of the remains to the United States. The disposition of remains is affected by local laws, customs, and facilities that are often vastly different from those in this country. The Bureau of Consular Affairs relays the family's instructions, and necessary private funds to cover the costs involved, to the embassy or consulate. The Department of State has no funds to assist in the return of remains or ashes of American citizens who die abroad. Upon completion of all formalities, the consular officer abroad prepares an official Foreign Service Report of Death, based upon the local death certificate, and sends it to the next of kin or legal representative for use in U.S. courts to settle estate matters.

A U.S. consular officer overseas has statutory responsibility for the personal estate of an American who dies abroad if the deceased has no legal representative in the country where the death occurred. The consular officer takes possession of personal effects, such as convertible assets, apparel, jewelry, personal documents, and papers. The officer prepares an inventory and then carries out instructions from members of the deceased's family concerning the effects. A final statement of the account is then sent to the next of kin. The diplomatic pouch cannot be used to ship personal items, including valuables, but legal documents and correspondence relating to the estate can be transmitted by pouch. In Washington, the Bureau of Consular Affairs gives the next of kin guidance on procedures to follow when preparing letters of administration, and affidavits of next of kin as acceptable evidence of legal claim of an estate.

Injury: When an American is injured abroad, the local embassy or consulate notifies the task force, which notifies family members in the United States. The Bureau of Consular Affairs can assist in sending private funds to the injured American. Frequently it collects information on the individual's prior medical history and forwards it to the embassy or consulate. When necessary, the State Department assists in arranging the return of the injured American to the United States commercially, with appropriate medical escort, via commercial air ambulance or, occasionally, by U.S. Air Force medical evacuation aircraft. The use of Air Force facilities for a medical evacuation is authorized only under certain stringent conditions, and when commercial evacuation is not possible. The full expense must be borne by the injured American or his family.

Evacuation: Sometimes commercial transportation entering and leaving a country is disrupted during a political upheaval or natural disaster. If this happens, and if it appears unsafe for Americans to remain, the embassy and consulates will work with the task force in Washington to charter special air flights and ground transportation to help Americans depart. The U.S. Government cannot order Americans to leave a foreign country. It can only advise and try to assist those who wish to leave.

The Privacy Act: The provisions of the Privacy Act of 1974 are designed to protect the privacy and rights of Americans, but occasionally they complicate efforts to assist citizens abroad. As a rule, consular officers may not reveal information regarding an individual American's location, welfare, intentions, or problems to anyone, including family members and congressional representatives, without the expressed consent of that individual. Although they may be sympathetic to the distress this can cause concerned families, consular officers must comply with the provisions of the Privacy Act.

(Bureau of Consular Affairs, U.S. Department of State)

What to Do When the Color-Coded Threat Levels Change

The Department of Homeland Security created the color-coded terrorism threat level system soon after the department was created. The system, intended as a warning to government and business, was simplified recently.

When there is credible information about a threat, an alert will be shared with the American public. It may include specific information, if available, about the nature of the threat, including the geographic region, mode of transportation, or critical infrastructure potentially affected by the threat, as well as steps that individuals and communities can take to protect themselves and help prevent, mitigate, or respond to the threat. The advisory will clearly indicate whether the threat is "Elevated," if we have no specific information about the timing or location, or "Imminent," if we believe the threat is impending/could potentially occur very soon.

Some common-sense advice for staying prepared:
• Maintain crisis plan protocols, including updates, training, and preventive procedures.
Yellow—Elevated
• Review physical security of all locations.
• Review access procedures for all visiting vehicles; consider an inspection procedure for all visiting vehicles.
• Remove trash containers and newspaper vending machines that could be used for bombs or other explosives.

• Monitor the media for possible incidents or additional warnings. Should an imminent threat be declared:

• Increase surveillance of critical locations.

• Take additional precautions at public events.

• Inspect all deliveries, including mail and messenger packages.

• Discontinue tours.

• Verify that all alternate worksites are ready for use if needed.

• Verify that all infrastructure at an alternate site is ready to operate.

• Restrict access to essential or cleared personnel only.

• Remove all vehicles from property unless owners are clearly identified.

Get to Know the Government

A complex array of documents and procedures has emerged from the Department of Homeland Security since its creation following 9/11. A veritable alphabet soup of procedures would require an entire book to explain the basics. These documents and procedures continue to emerge and will be with us for the foreseeable future. While they are complex and often Byzantine, they should not be ignored. The simple fact is that in an emergency of severe proportions, they will affect the actions and outcomes of private enterprise.

The National Response Plan alone is comprised of five complex elements: the Domestic Readiness Group, coordinated by the White House; the Incident Advisory Council; the National Operations Center; the Strategic Information Operations Center; and the Principal Federal Official.

In the event of a severe emergency:

• You may lose some or all control over your operations.

• You may be called upon to contribute necessary items and services to an impacted area.

Become familiar with some of the central documents—specifically the National Response Plan and the National Incident Management System. They are complex documents that spell out, in theory at least, what might occur during an extreme event.

Get to know your local government resources and what they can and cannot do. In a crisis, details and resources count. For example, if you have operations in suburban or smaller townships and you require a bomb squad to take over a suspicious package, do not assume the local government has a bomb squad —or if it does, that it can handle more than one call at a time. If you know that in advance of any event, you would be wise to have a commercial bomb squad on tap.

Finally—What can you do to make this all work?

As mentioned earlier, the goal for any company, regardless of size, should be to have a senior executive, or possibly two or three co-equals, reporting to the CEO, responsible for crisis readiness and response. At forward-acting companies and others that are not quite prepared yet, a smart practice would be to create a crisis planning committee. The committee, with senior executives representing key departments on the crisis team, would have oversight for the crisis readiness-and-response strategy, and in particular responsibility for carrying out/following through on the lessons learned from each simulation and actual crisis.

12: Ideas Beyond the Norm or "Why Aren't We Doing That?"

Grief or Assistance?

All too often we hear, in the wake of a tragedy, that the company or organization is providing "grief counselors." Grief is a very private emotion, and it is difficult to believe that employees or customers who have been involved in a life-threatening or tragic experience want to meet total strangers who—though qualified—will begin soothing their grief as if they were their own clergymen, analysts, or close friends. What people really need in the wake of these experiences is assistance—with transportation, medical care, and the countless other details they may face. You would be well served to consider, in lieu of or in addition to the "grief counselors," experienced assistance teams that can help smooth the way during a difficult period. Not coincidentally, the better the assistance, the less likelihood of lawsuits and lingering anger.

The Devil's in the Details

In a disaster, when power is lost, cell phones will become indispensable—until they need recharging. A few devices are now on the market that provide battery charges or boosters for cell phones, another essential part of the emergency supply room.

Don't give up on all the traditional landline phones. Have at least one in the house in case the local cells go down.

And ATMs operate on electricity. So have some cash on hand.

Remind employees to designate a friend or family member outside the crisis area as a central contact, so that others in the family can contact that one person for news.

Broaden the Scope of Crisis Training

Israel's Egged Bus Company prepares for contingencies by training key employees to be able to take over another completely different job if needed in an emergency. The concept, called multiskilled training, Egged reports, has other benefits, creating new friendships, a stronger sense of their individual value, and greater appreciation of the big picture.

An Expiration Date

We all know that crisis plans need to be kept up to date. A stale plan is useless. One way to remind all that the plan needs to be updated is to post a prominent expiration date on the plan. Imagine picking up a plan with an expired date when a crisis hits. It will not occur twice.

An Invitation to Government

Add a new dimension to your simulations by inviting local government representatives to observe them. Emergency management authorities from police to fire to the mayor's office can gain a greater understanding of your business and crisis plans, and add valuable perspective during the debrief.

Won't a Video Solve all the Problems?

A common question:

"I have no time for crisis drills," say some CEOs, "no matter how much you try to convince me. So I made a great video telling everyone in the company how important it to be crisis-ready. Isn't that enough?"

No. A video, no matter how well produced it is and how compelling you are, is window dressing. It may make you feel as though you've done something, but you really haven't. Five minutes after the mandatory screening for all employees, everyone goes back to work and forgets it. What really counts is a commitment and program where plans are created and tested.

A Fresh Approach to Risk Assessment

Go beyond the basics and ask some tough questions: If you were an ex-employee with complete freedom to say what you wanted to say, what risks would you list? And if you were an investigative journalist turned loose inside the company, what risks would you find?

Emergency Supplies

When preparing for emergency situations, it's best to think first about the basics of survival: fresh water, food, clean air, and warmth. Encourage everyone to have a portable kit customized to meet their personal needs, with essential medications and two battery-powered radios. A commercial radio is a good source for news and information from local authorities. A NOAA weather radio can alert you to weather emergencies or announcements from the Department of Homeland Security. Get one with a tone-alert feature, if possible, which automatically alerts you when a watch or warning is issued in your area. (Tone-alert is not available in some areas.) Include extra batteries.

In addition to electronic files, keep copies of important records such as site maps, building plans, insurance policies, employee contact and identification information, bank account records, supplier and shipping contact lists, computer backups, emergency or law enforcement contact information, and other priority documents in a waterproof, fireproof portable container. Store a duplicate set at an off-site location.

Talk to your co-workers about what emergency supplies the company can feasibly provide, if any, and which ones individuals should consider keeping on hand.

Recommended emergency supplies include the following:
• One gallon of water per person per day, for drinking and sanitation
• Food, at least a three-day supply of non-perishable food
• Battery-powered radio and extra batteries
• Flashlight and extra batteries
• First-aid kits
• Whistles to signal for help
• Dust or filter masks, readily available in hardware stores, which are rated based on how small a particle they filter out
• Moist towelettes for sanitation

- Wrenches or pliers to turn off utilities
- Can openers for food (if kit contains canned food)
- Plastic sheeting and duct tape to seal rooms
- Garbage bags and plastic ties for personal sanitation

Budgeting for Preparedness

Ready.gov, the Department of Homeland Security's business preparedness guide, has constructed an interesting budget worksheet on preparedness.

No Cost
- Meet with your insurance provider to review current coverage.
- Create procedures to quickly evacuate and also to shelter in place. Practice the plans.
- Talk to staff about the company's disaster plans. Two-way communication is central before, during, and after a disaster.
- Create an emergency contact list, including employee emergency contact information.
- Create a list of critical business contractors and others whom you will need in an emergency.
- Know what kinds of emergencies might affect your company both internally and externally.
- Decide in advance what you will do if your building is unusable.
- Create a list of inventory and equipment—including computer hardware, software and peripherals—for insurance purposes.
- Talk to utility service providers about potential alternatives, and identify backup options.
- Promote family and individual preparedness among your coworkers.
- Include emergency preparedness information during staff meetings, in newsletters, on the company intranet, in periodic employee e-mails, and via other internal communications methods.

Under $500
- Buy a fire extinguisher and smoke alarm.

- Set up a telephone call tree, a password-protected page on the company website, an e-mail alert, or a call-in voice recording to communicate with employees during an emergency.
- Provide first-aid and CPR training to key employees.
- Use and keep up to date antivirus software and firewalls.
- Attach equipment and cabinets to walls or to other, more stable, equipment.
- Place heavy or breakable objects on low shelves.
- Elevate valuable inventory and electric machinery off the floor in case of flooding.
- Make sure your building's HVAC system is working properly and is well maintained.
- Back up your records and critical data. Keep a copy offsite.

More than $500
- Consider additional insurance such as business interruption, flood, or earthquake policies.
- Purchase, install, and pre-wire a generator to the building's essential electrical circuits. Provide for other utility alternatives and backup options.
- Install automatic sprinkler systems, fire hoses, and fire-resistant doors and walls.
- Make sure your building meets all current standards and codes. Consider a professional engineer to evaluate the wind, fire, or seismic resistance of your building.
- Consider a security professional to evaluate and/or create your disaster-preparedness and business-continuity plan.
- Upgrade your building's HVAC system to secure outdoor air intakes and increase filter efficiency.
- Send safety and key emergency response employees to training programs or conferences.
- Provide a large group of employees with first aid and CPR training.

Steps easily taken in many locations:
- Installation of curbside barriers that would prevent access to buildings by car and truck bombs.
- Tightening of security in commercial garages.

• Implementation of visitor security systems that really screen people. While many buildings in New York City, for example, have implemented tight systems, a vast number of office buildings around the United States have visitor sign-in procedures that simply require a signature, legible or not. Nothing else.

Keep the Evacuation Drills Realistic

Every real evacuation has surprises. When planning an evacuation drill, build in an element of surprise—block an escape route; add a number of visitors.

Remember to test the PA system—can everyone hear the signals and the announcements?

Subscribe!

The best publication in crisis management and business continuity is *Continuity Central*, published in London. This free online newsletter is published weekly and, despite its title that gives the impression that it is about business continuity, it covers the entire international crisis management field, with announcements, reports, and surveys. Highly recommended. To subscribe, log on to *www.continuitycentral.com*.

Join!

The Business Continuity Institute (BCI) is a well-established organization offering guidance and support from fellow business continuity practitioners.

Through its certification program, the institute provides internationally recognized status to its members, as professional membership in the BCI demonstrates the members' competence to carry out business continuity management to a consistent high standard. The BCI has over three thousand members in seventy-five-plus countries.

The wider role of the BCI is to promote the highest standards of professional competence and commercial ethics in the provision and maintenance of business-continuity planning and services. Contact them at *www.thebci.org*.

Index

9/11 viii 3 4 16 27 28 30 63 64 66 78 92
A
Achille Lauro 41
Air Florida 51
All-hazards 19 105
American Airlines 24 60 84 113
American Heritage Dictionary 75
American Red Cross 66
Apology 75 76 77
Argenti, Paul 28 29 113
Augustine, Norman 66 72

B
BellSouth 24
Bhopal 59
Biotechnology Industry Organization 98
Blog 86 103
Bloggers 83
Blogging 86
Bloomberg, Michael viii 30 34 35
Boston University 78
Boycott 98 99
Bridging 103 104 124
British Petroleum 1
Budgeting for Preparedness 140
Bureau of Consular Affairs 132 133 134
Burke, Jim v vii 15 43 44 46 47 51 72 77 87
Burson, Harold vii 18
Business Continuity viii 4 5 27 31 36 92 103 109 112 116 117 130 143
Business Continuity Institute 143
Business Roundtable 96

C
Call Tree 103 141
Carrison, Dan 17
Central Intelligence Agency 106
Charisma 77 78
Chicago River 55
Churchill, Winston 71
CNN 18 23 24 26 32 83 84 85 87 114 123
Coca-Cola 50
Collins, Jim 46
Color-Coded Threat Levels 134
Columbia University 18 23 32
CommCore Consulting Group 47
Compaq 56
Consumer Reports 66
Continuity Central 71 117 143
Crisis Team 2 28 68 73 74 103 107 108 111 112 113
114 116 121 122 130 136
Customers v vii viii 18 20 29 33 45 47 49 54 55 65
71 72 76 77 86 87 108 109 113 116 117 129 131
137

D
Dalkon Shield 56
Dartmouth 28 71
Davis, Evelyn Y. 97
Densen, Rob 29
Department of Homeland Security 10 11 35 67 92 93 103
105 106 117 119 134 135 139 140
Dirty Bomb 104
Drucker, Peter 72 73 95
Duke University 77
Dunn, Patricia 56

E
Economist, The 63
Emergency Supplies 25 139
Employees 18 20 21 24 25 26 28 29 45 49 51 55 56

57 68 70 71 72 74 75 76 95 96 108 109 112 113
114 116 117 119 121 124 127 128 129 131 137 138
141
Enron ix 15 56 57
Environmental Protection Agency 53
Exxon Valdez 51 53 76 99

F
FedEx 25 26 30 114
Fiorina, Carly 56
Firestone 58
Florida State University 70
Folgers 24
Food and Drug Administration 44 47
Ford 58
Foresman, George 67
Fuqua School of Business 77

G

General Motors 58
Gerber 48 49
GETS Cards 104
Gilman v 47 77 78
Girl Scout cookies 48
Giuliani, Rudy viii 11 23 28 71 78
Grace, Nancy 83
Grove, Andy 4 54 55

H
Halpern, Danny 17
Hazelwood, Ed 52
Hewlett-Packard 56
Hill & Knowlton 21
Hochwarter 70
Holdeman, Eric 19
Home Depot 22 24 71 97
Homeland Security 10 11 12 35 67 92 93 103 104 105
106 117 119 134 135 139 140

Homeland Security Council 11   12
Hopgood, Suzanne v   93   94   95
Houston, Whitney 82
Hubris 56   57
Hurricane Katrina 2   24   32   67   70

I
Iarossi, Frank 51   52
IBM 54
Immelt, Jeff 71   73
Incident Commander 104
Incident of National Significance 104
Intel 54
International Apple Institute 53
International Crisis Management Institute 91   93
International Standards Organization 92   104
Interoperability 104
ISACs 105
Ismay, J. Bruce 40

J
JetBlue 61
Johnson, Jr. vii 15   43   45   46   77
Johnson & Johnson vii 15   43   45   46   77
Joint Field Office 105

K
Kaplan, Eyal 17
Katrina 2   4   12   15   23   24   25   26   27   29   32   67   70   128
129
Kellerman, Barbara 76   77
Kennedy, Donald 9   55
Kessler, Dr. David 48
Klinghoffer, Leon 41
Kniffen, Robert 44
Korn/Ferry 16
Kozlowski, Dennis 57   58
Kramer, Jim 84

Kurtz, Howard 83   84

L
Leber, Jonathan 59
Lindell, Michael 28
Lockheed Martin 66
Louisiana State University 27
Lynchburg College 54

M
McDonald's 22
MCI ix
Menu Foods 59

N
NACD Blue Ribbon Commission on Risk Oversight 22   93   94
Nardelli, Bob 22   71   97
National Cancer Institute 53
National Center for Disaster Preparedness 18   23   32
National Fire Protection Association 66   92   105
National Heart Savers Association 22
National Incident Management System 105   135
National Infrastructure Protection Plan 105
National Response Plan 105   135
Navarro, Peter 63
New Media Strategies 86
NewsHour 83   85
NFPA 28   66   92   93   96   105   106
Nicely, Thomas 54
Nissan 58
NOAA 114   139

P
Palestine Liberation Front 41
Parenio, Sue 78
Parks, Rosa 98
Patriot Act 106
PBS 82   83   85

Pentium Chips 54
People for the Ethical Treatment of Animals 98
Pepsi 48 49
Perrier 50
Pet Food Recall 58
Pew Research Center xii
Privacy Act 134

R
Rawl, Lawrence 51 52 87
Ready.gov 35 92 106 140
Redlener, Dr. Irwin 18 23 32
Risk communication 20 96 106
Robins, A.H. 15 56

S
Shelter in Place 106 140
Simulated Press Conference 122
Simulation 28 65 107 108 122 123 130 136
Sixty Minutes 76
Snyder, Pete 86
Stanford University 55
State Department 131 132 133
Steinberg, Howard 97
Stossel, John 47

T
Tabletop Exercise 122
Tankersley, Michael W. 93 94 95
Terrorist Threat Integration Center 106
Texas A&M University 28
Thatcher, Margaret 27
Threat Levels, Color-Coded 134
Three Mile Island 60
Titanic 39 40 41
Today Show 87
TOPOFF 106
Townsend, Frances Frago 19

Travel 63 81 113 128 131
Triangle 24 42
Tuck School of Business 28
Tyco ix 15 56 57
Tylenol vii viii 1 15 43 44 46 47 48 49 50 51 60 77 87 110

U
Union Carbide 15 59 60
University of California 63
University of New Orleans 27
UPS viii 30
USA Today 11 61

W
Wagner, Tim 84
Walden Israel Venture Capital 17
Wall Street Journal 54 56 71 81 83 126
Walmart 16 24
War Room viii 113
Welch, Jack and Suzy 4 19 43 71 73 96
White Star Line 40
Whitley, Joseph D. 92
Whitworth, Ralph V. 97
Wikipedia 86 103
Wilcox, John 98

For sales, editorial information, subsidiary rights information
or a catalog, please write or phone or e-mail
Brick Tower Press
1230 Park Avenue, 9a
New York, NY 10128, US
Sales: 1-800-68-BRICK
Tel: 212-427-7139
www.BrickTowerPress.com
bricktower@aol.com

www.Ingram.com

For sales in the UK and Europe please contact our distributor,
Gazelle Book Services
Falcon House, Queens Square
Lancaster, LA1 1RN, UK
Tel: (01524) 68765 Fax: (01524) 63232
stef@gazellebooks.co.uk

www.ingramcontent.com/pod-product-compliance
Lightning Source LLC
Chambersburg PA
CBHW071555200326
41519CB00021BB/6756